This Book Belongs to

puzzle 1

puzzle 2

puzzle 3

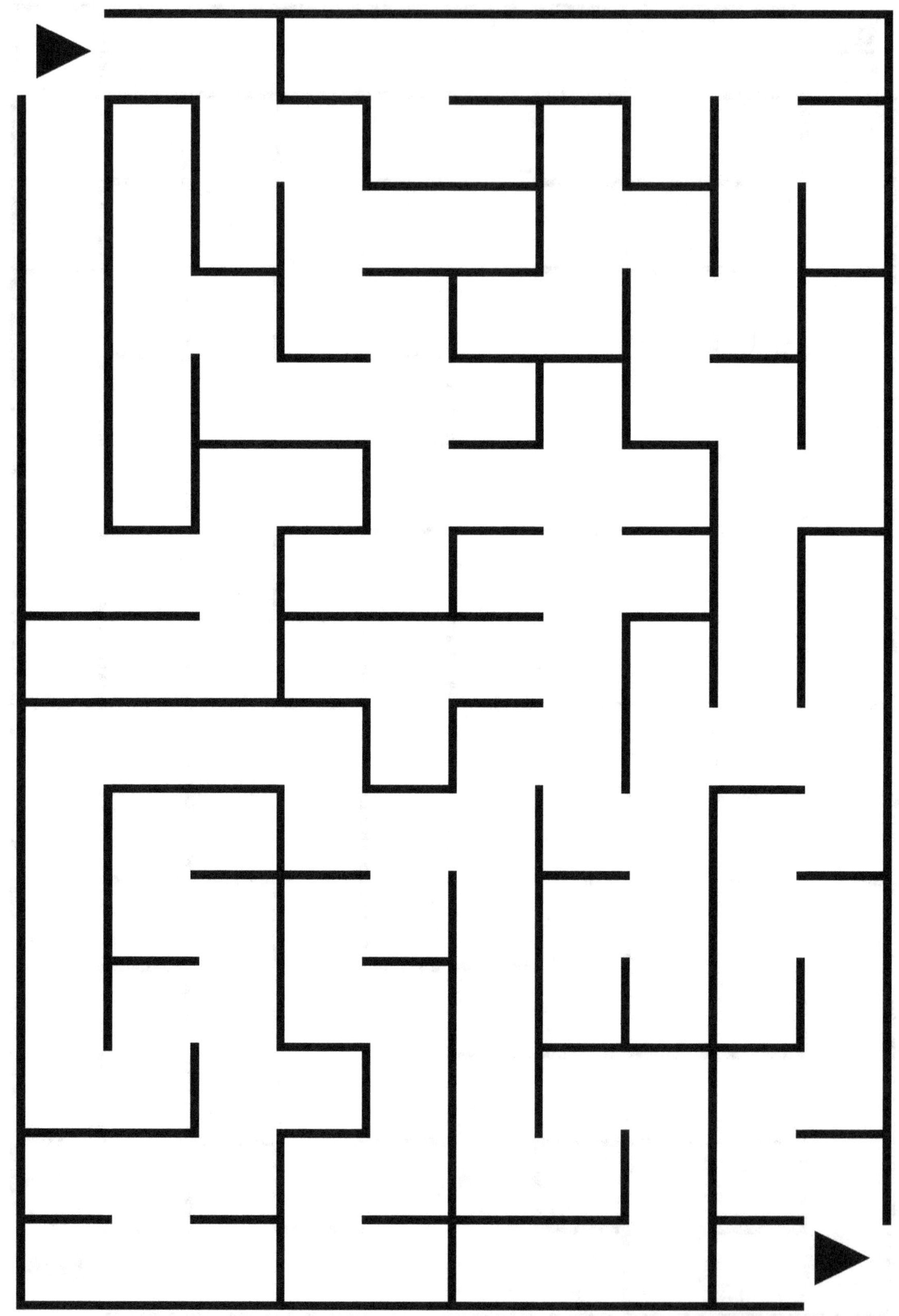

puzzle 4

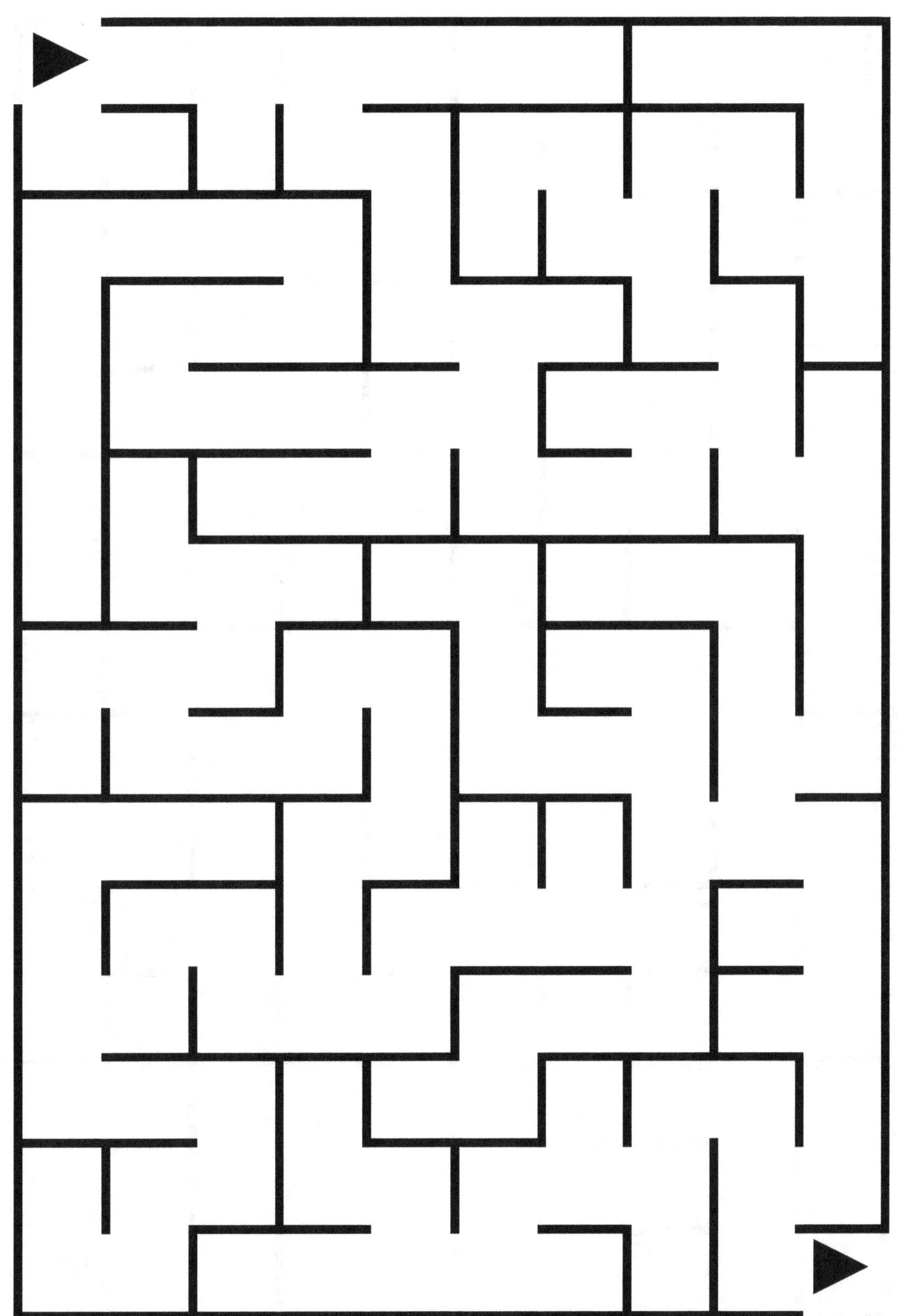

puzzle 5

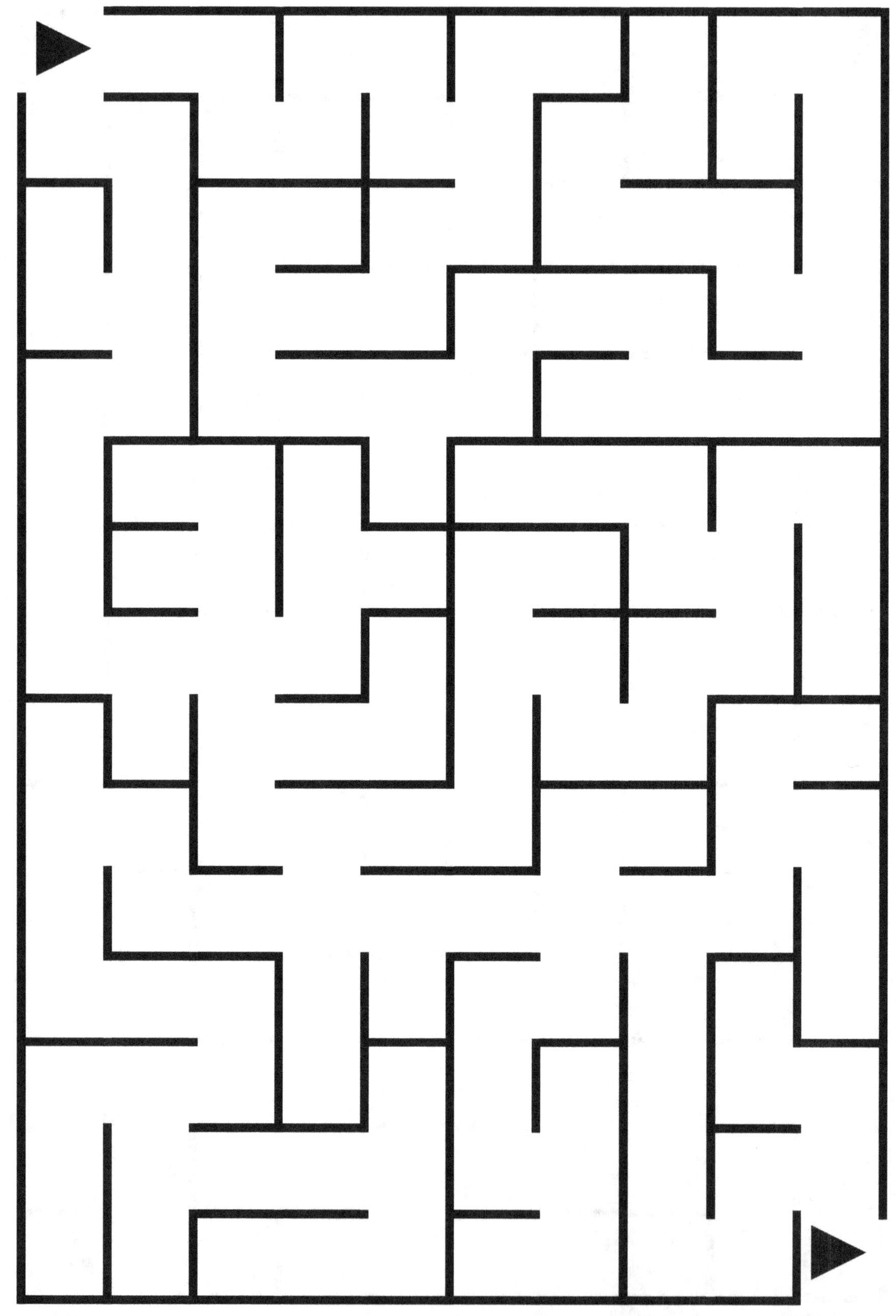

puzzle 6

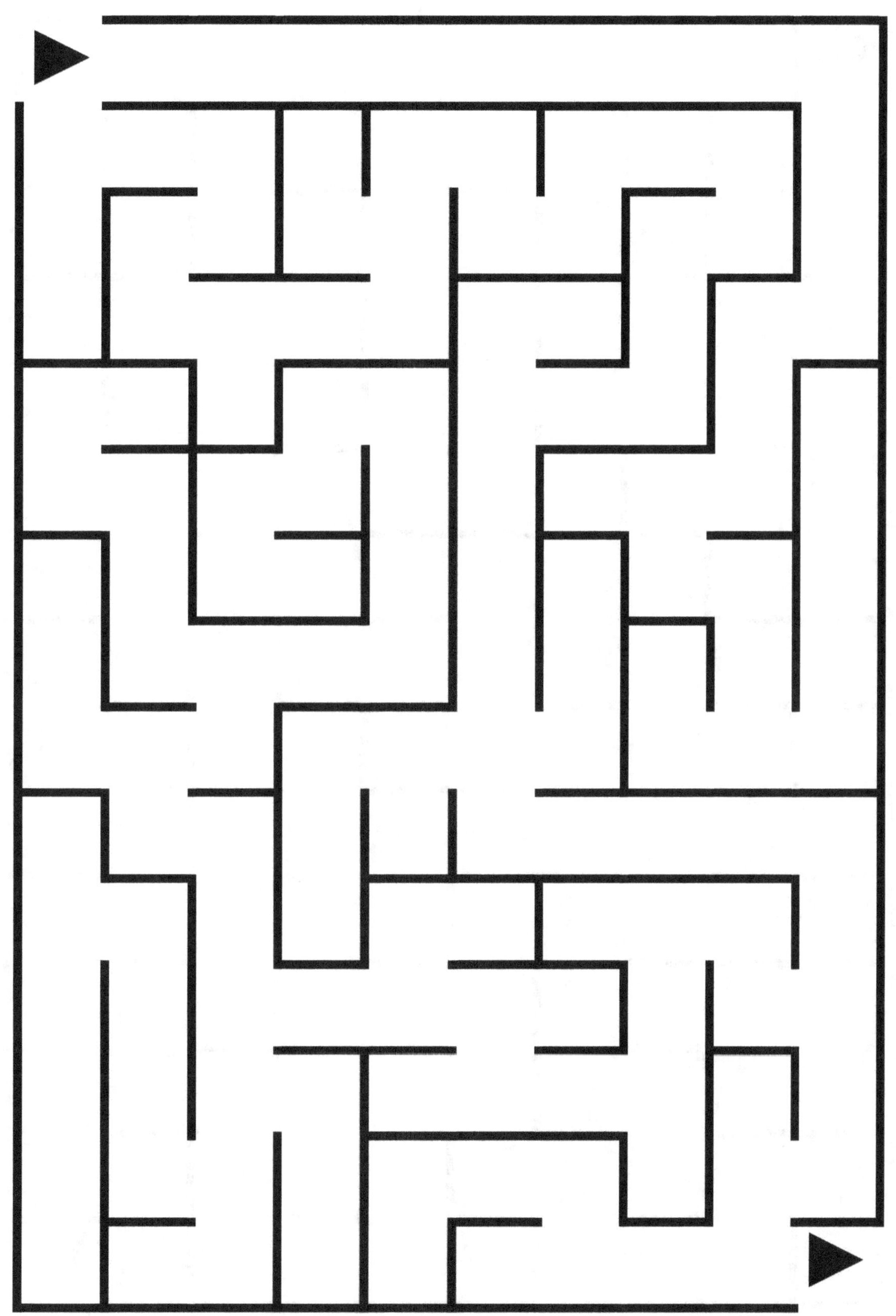

puzzle 7

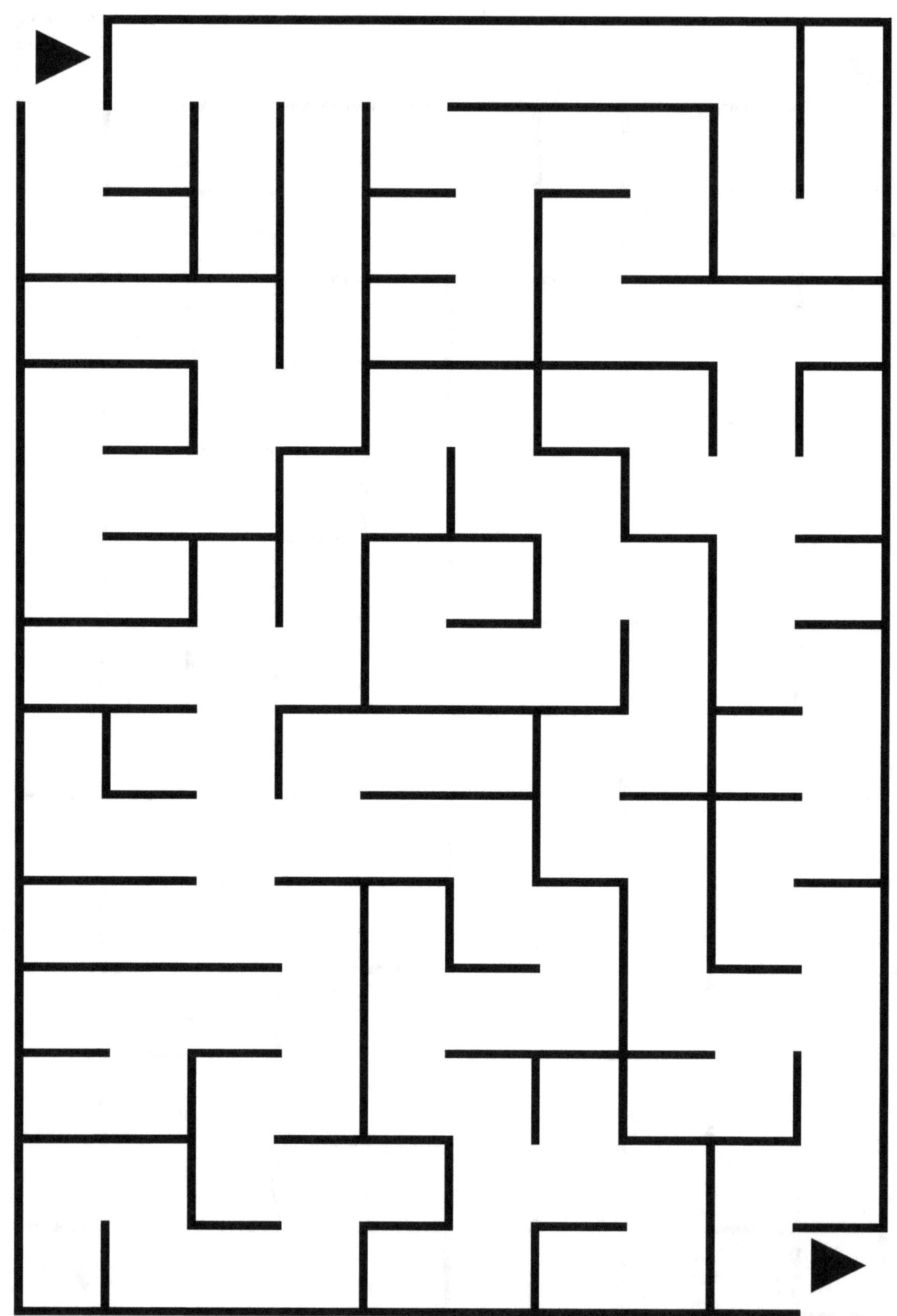

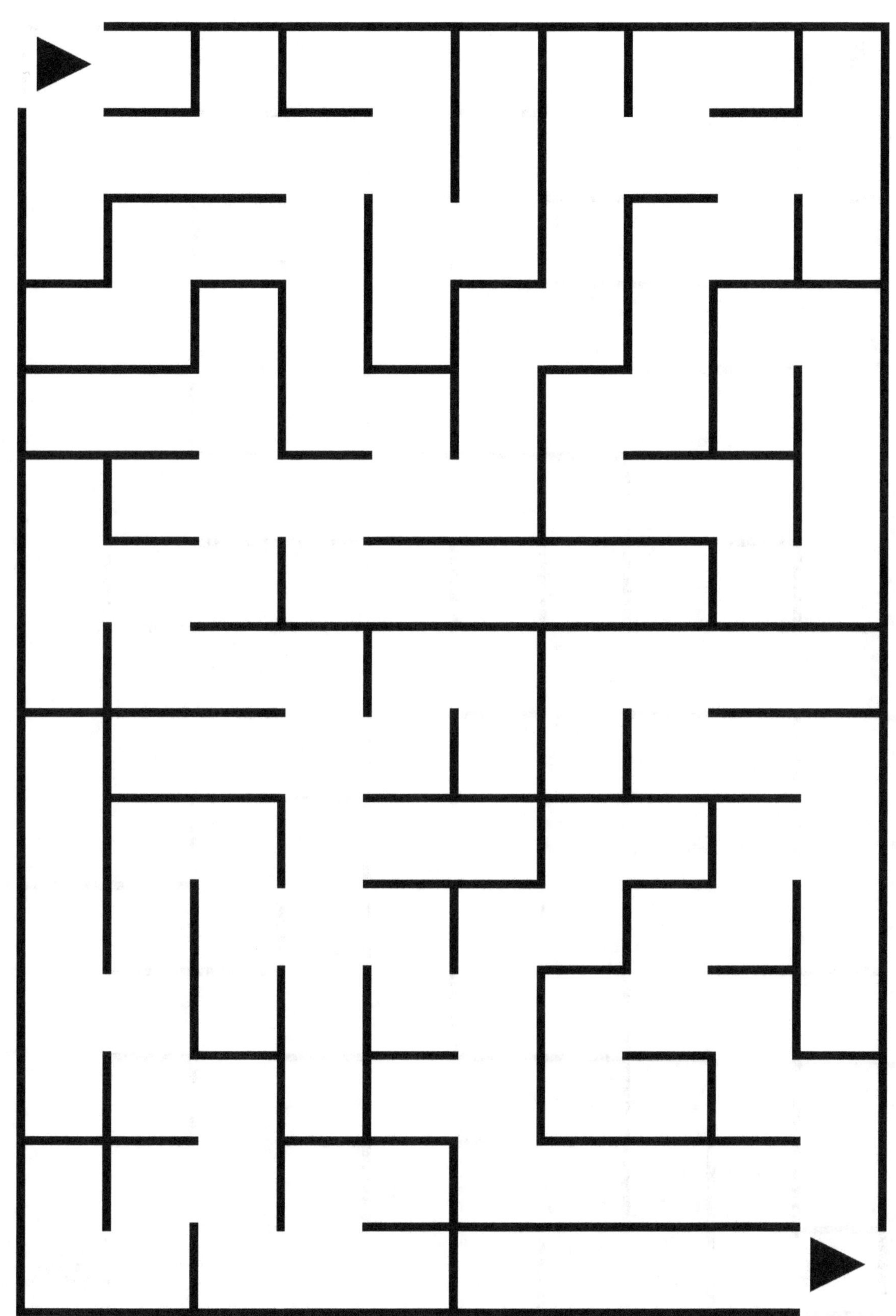

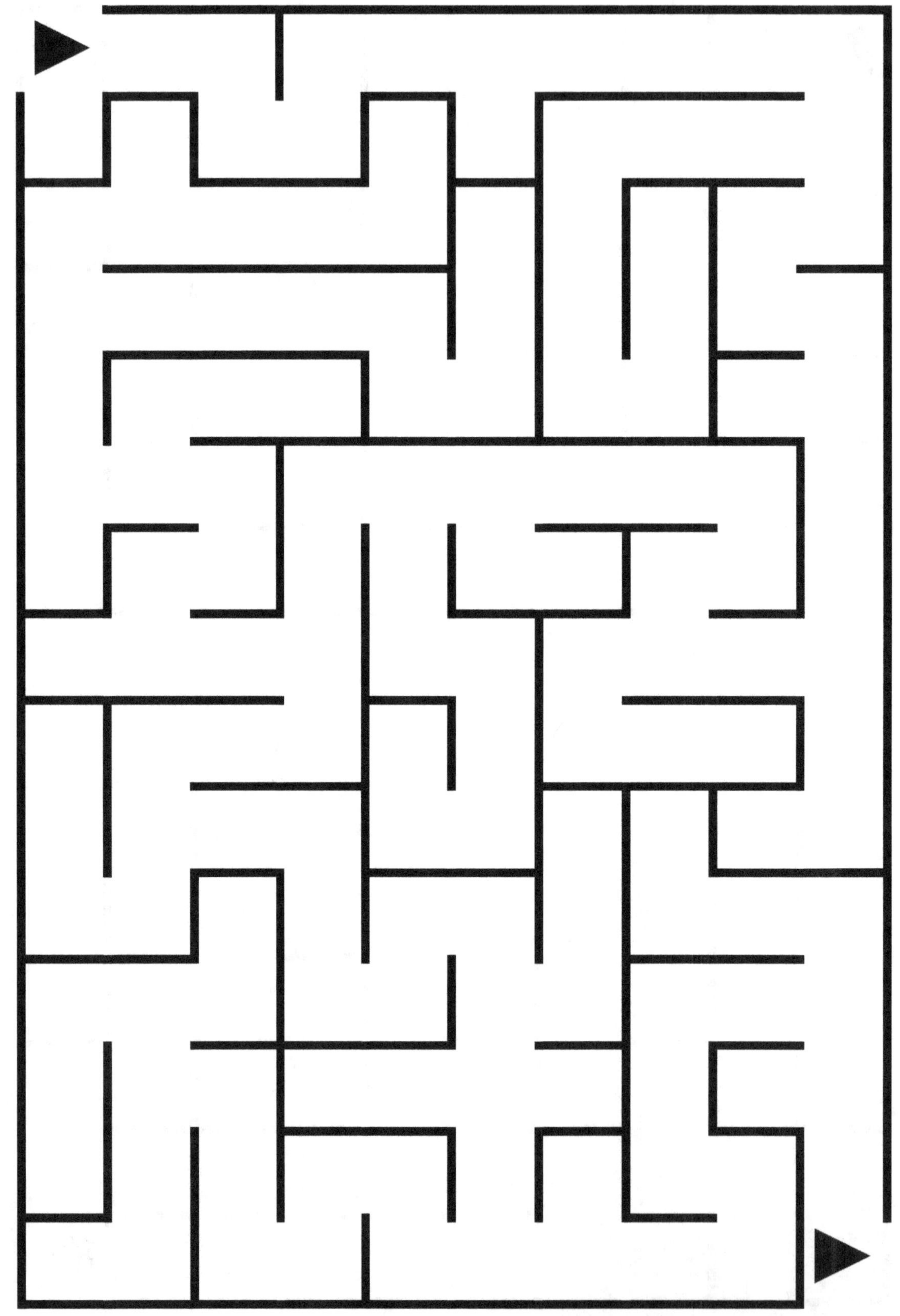

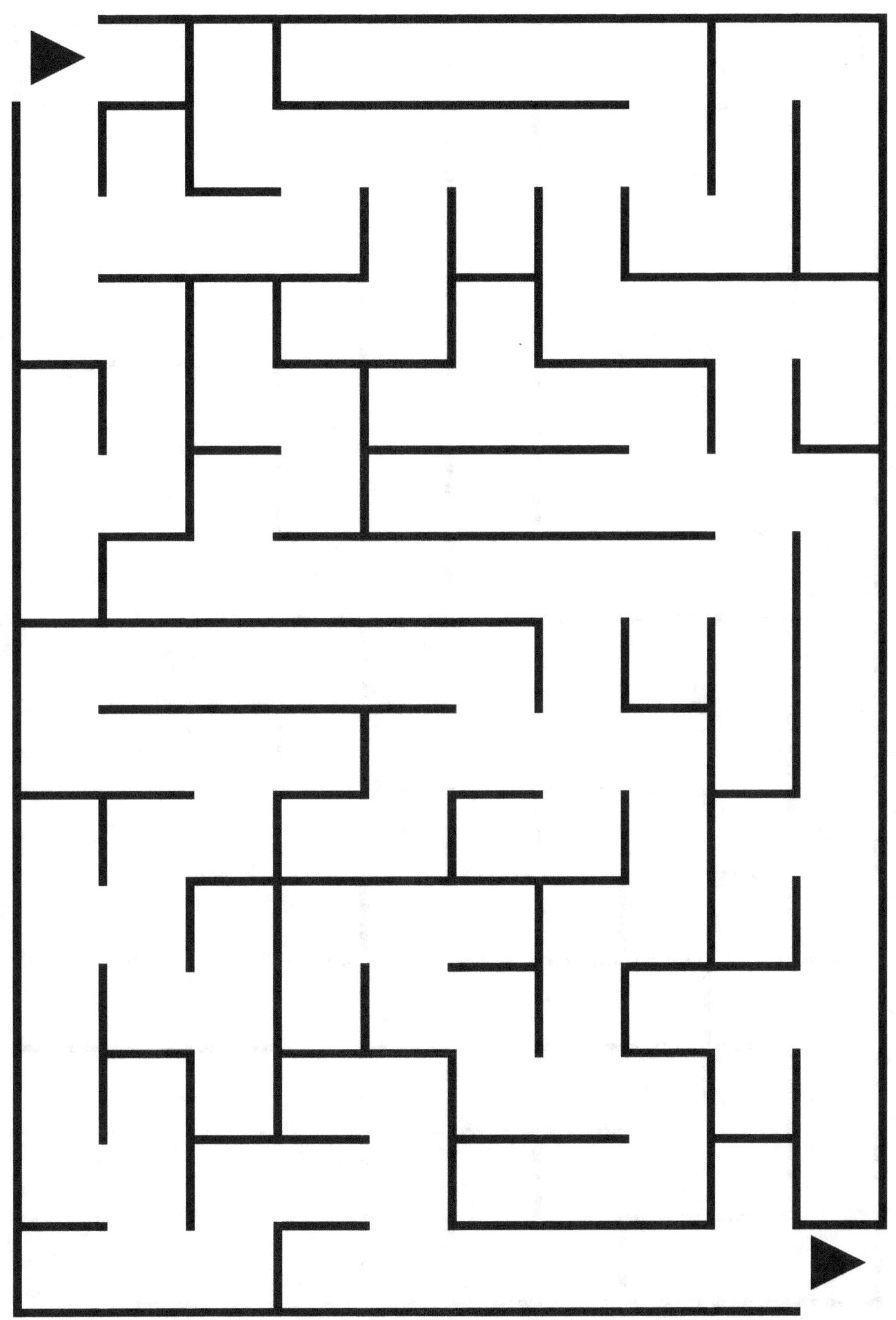

puzzle 11

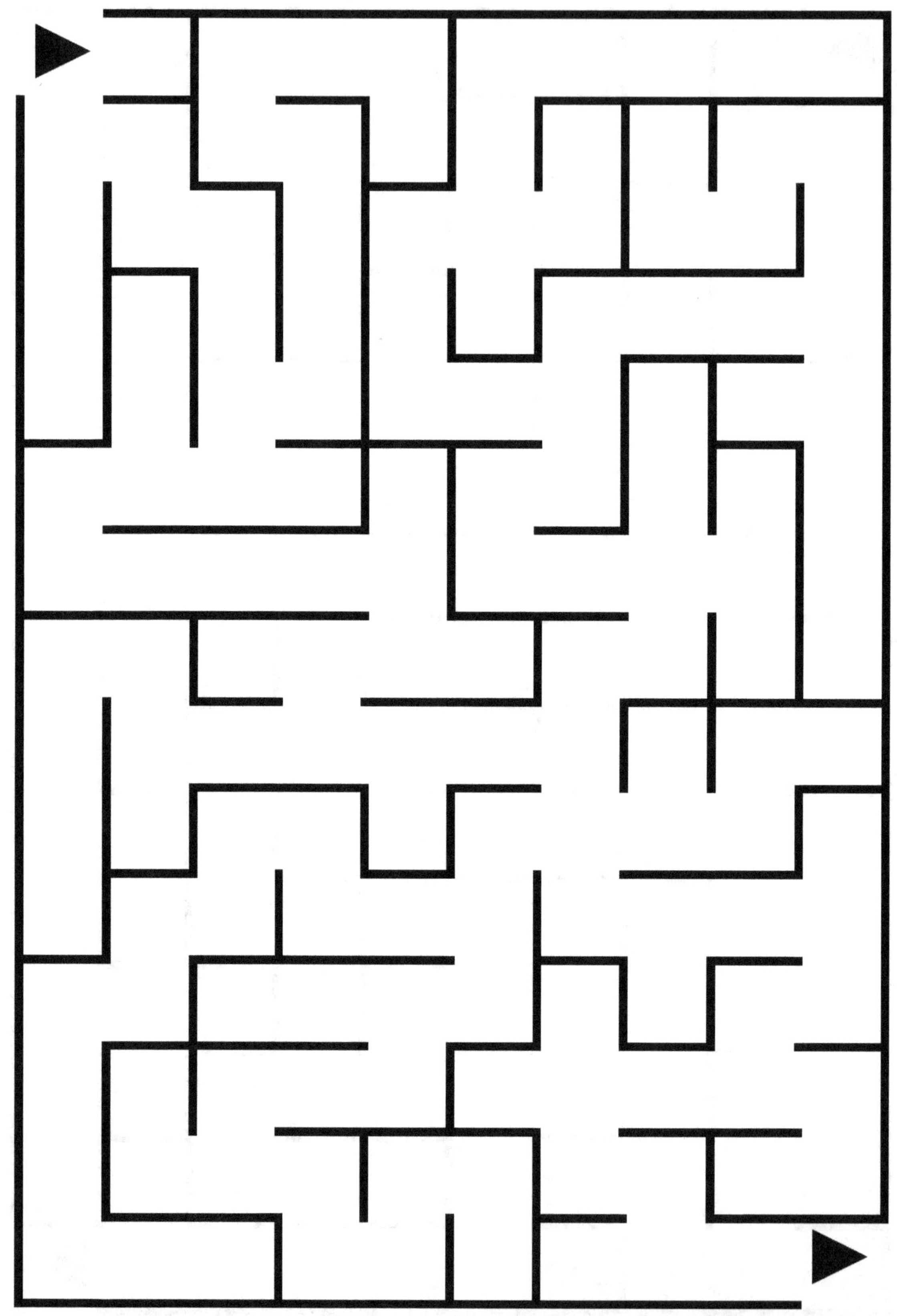

puzzle 12

puzzle 13

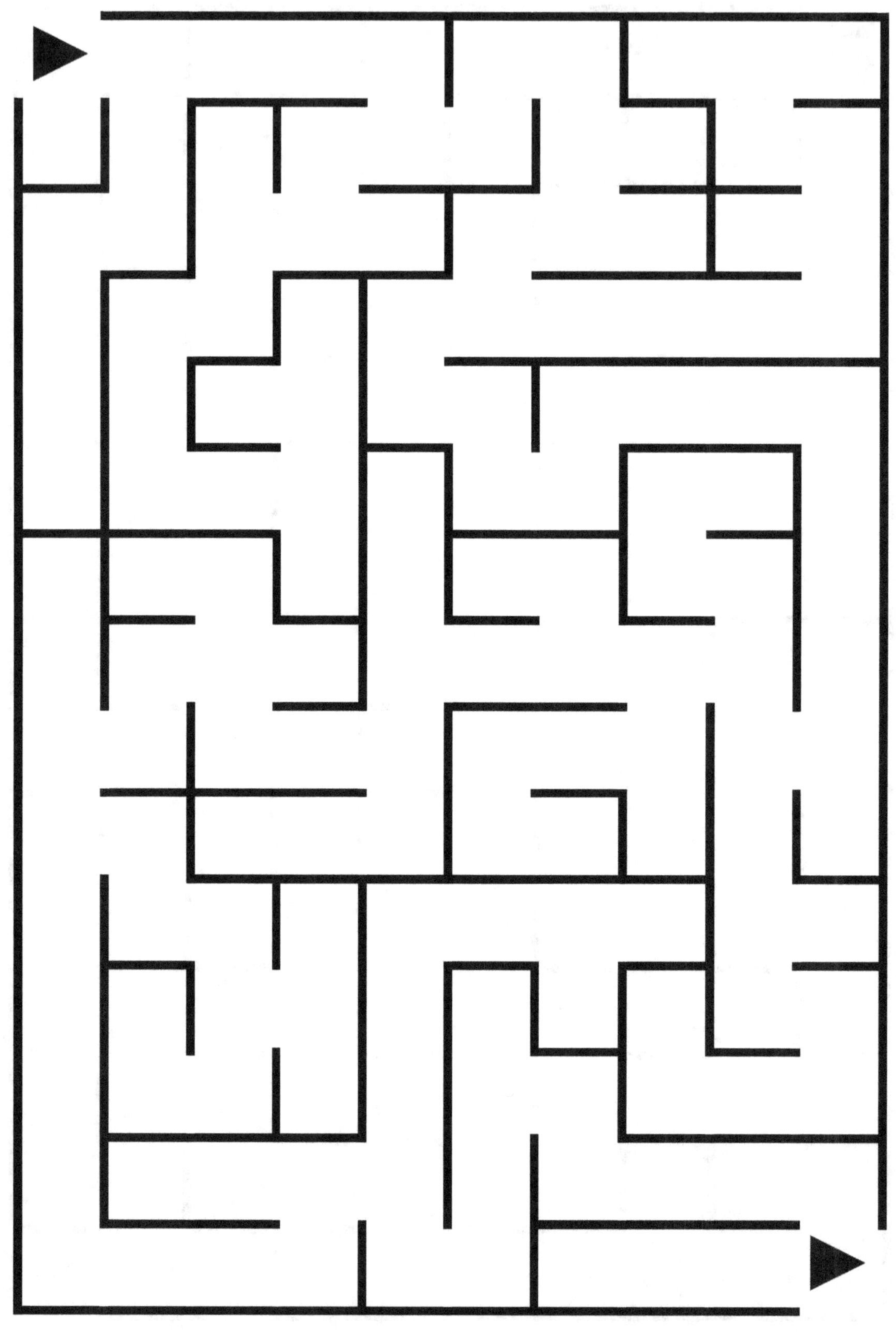

puzzle 14

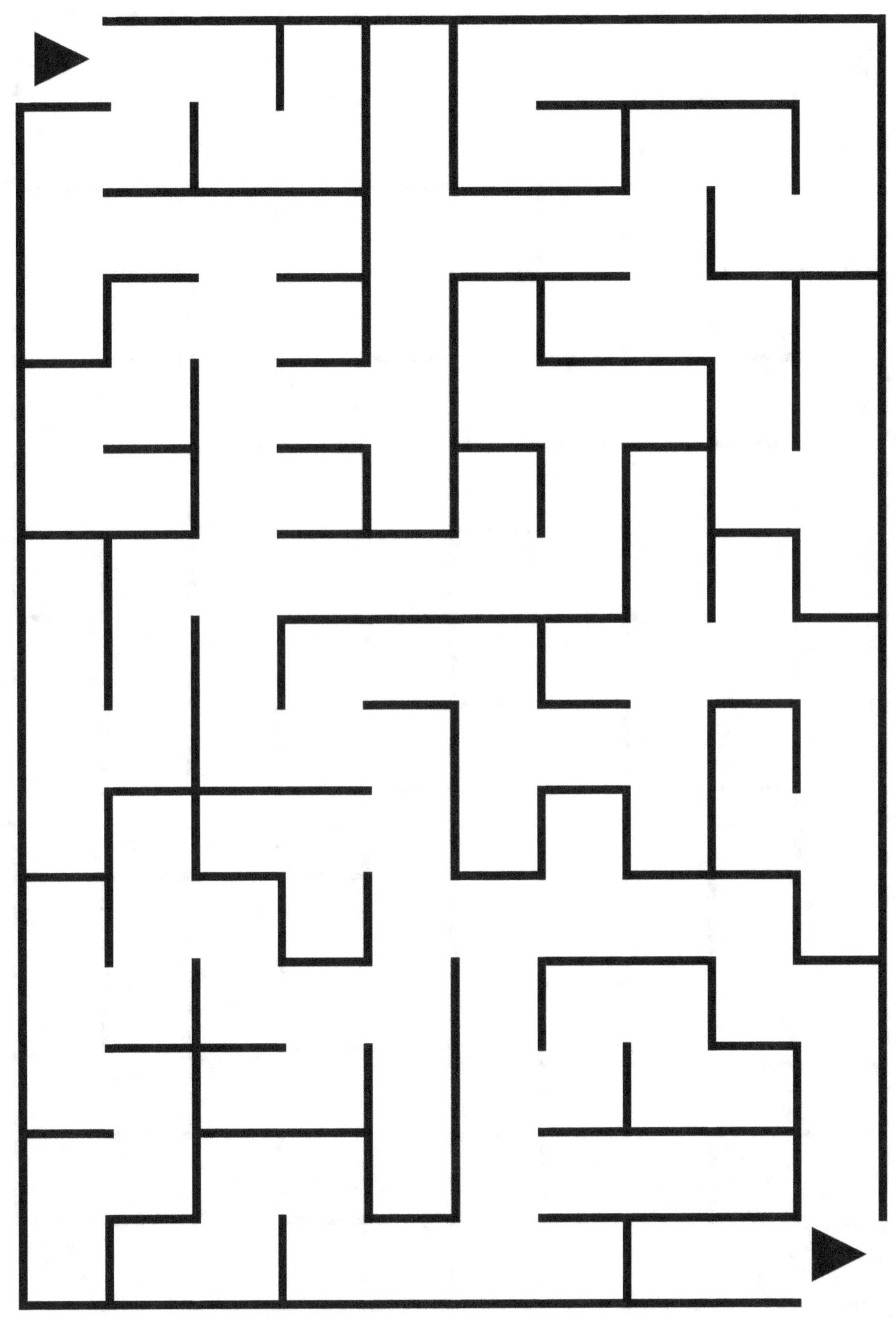

puzzle 15

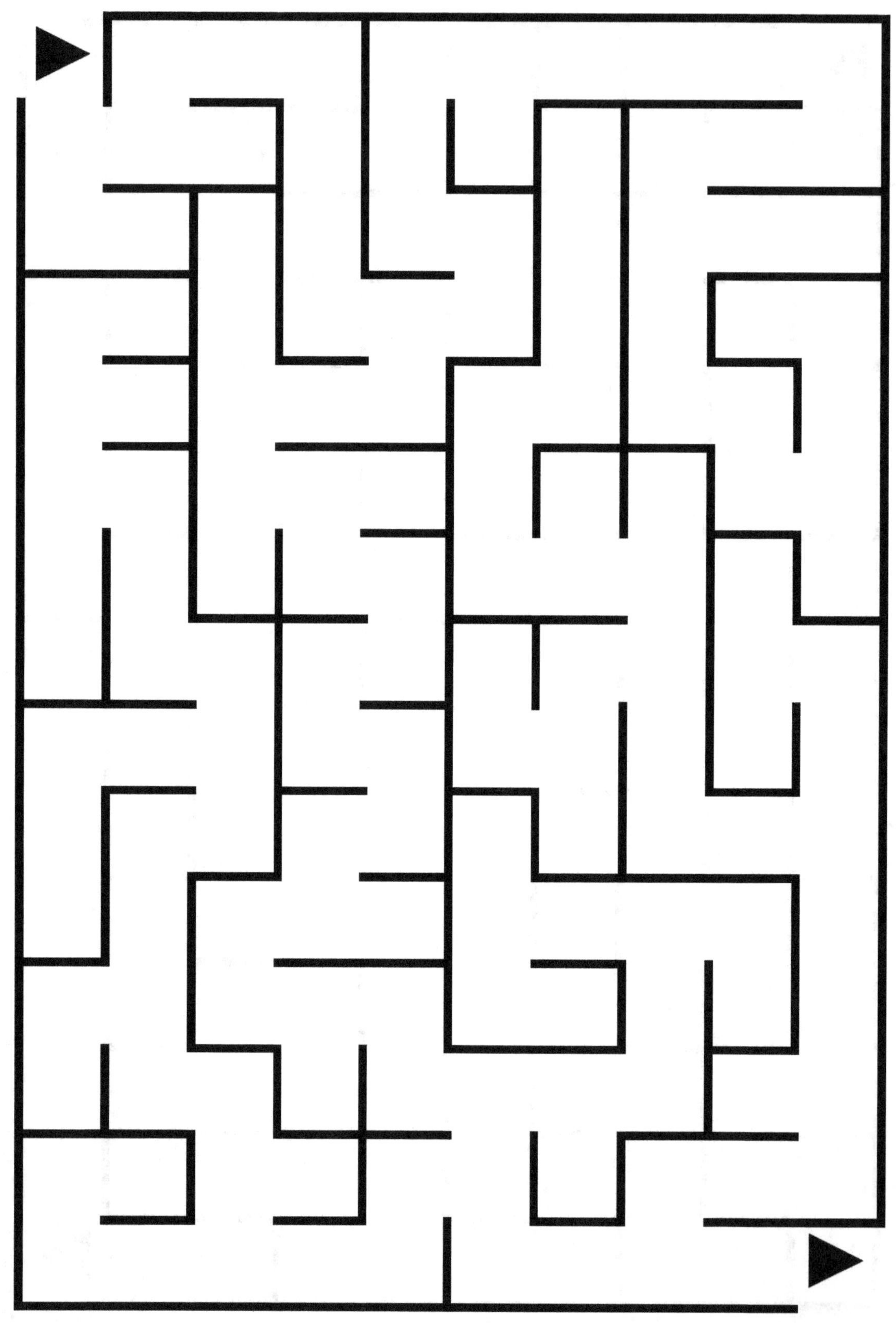

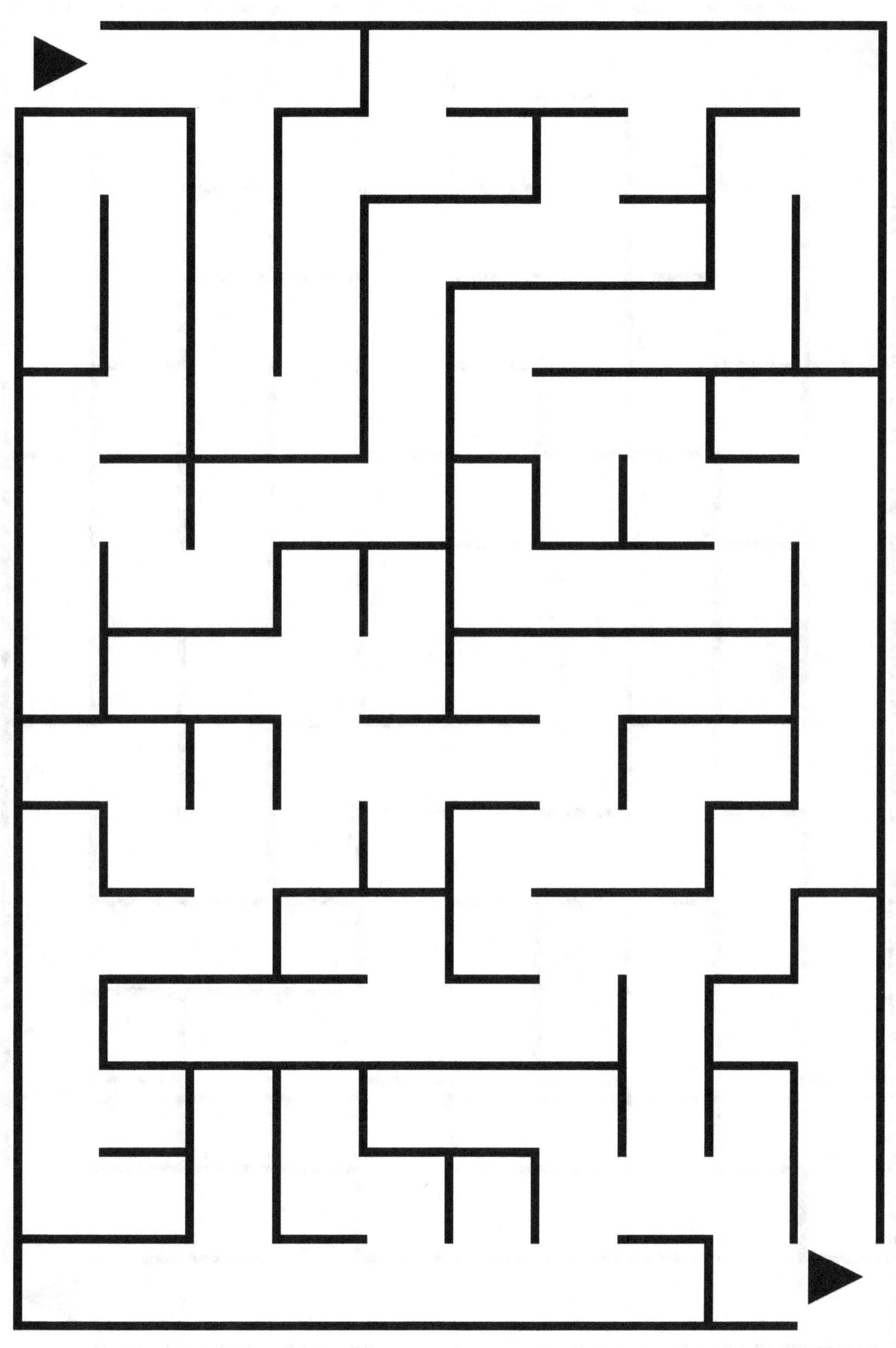

puzzle 17

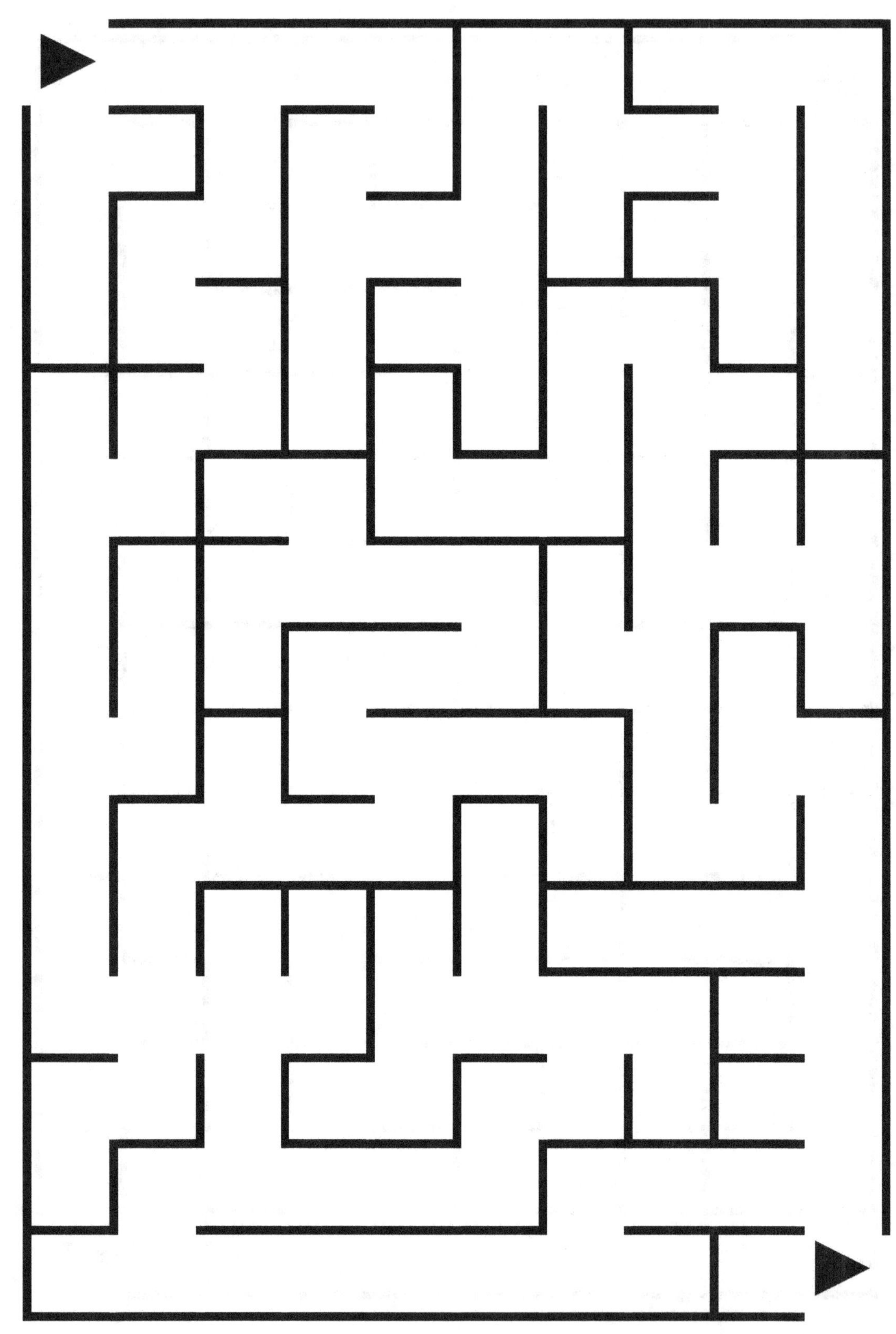

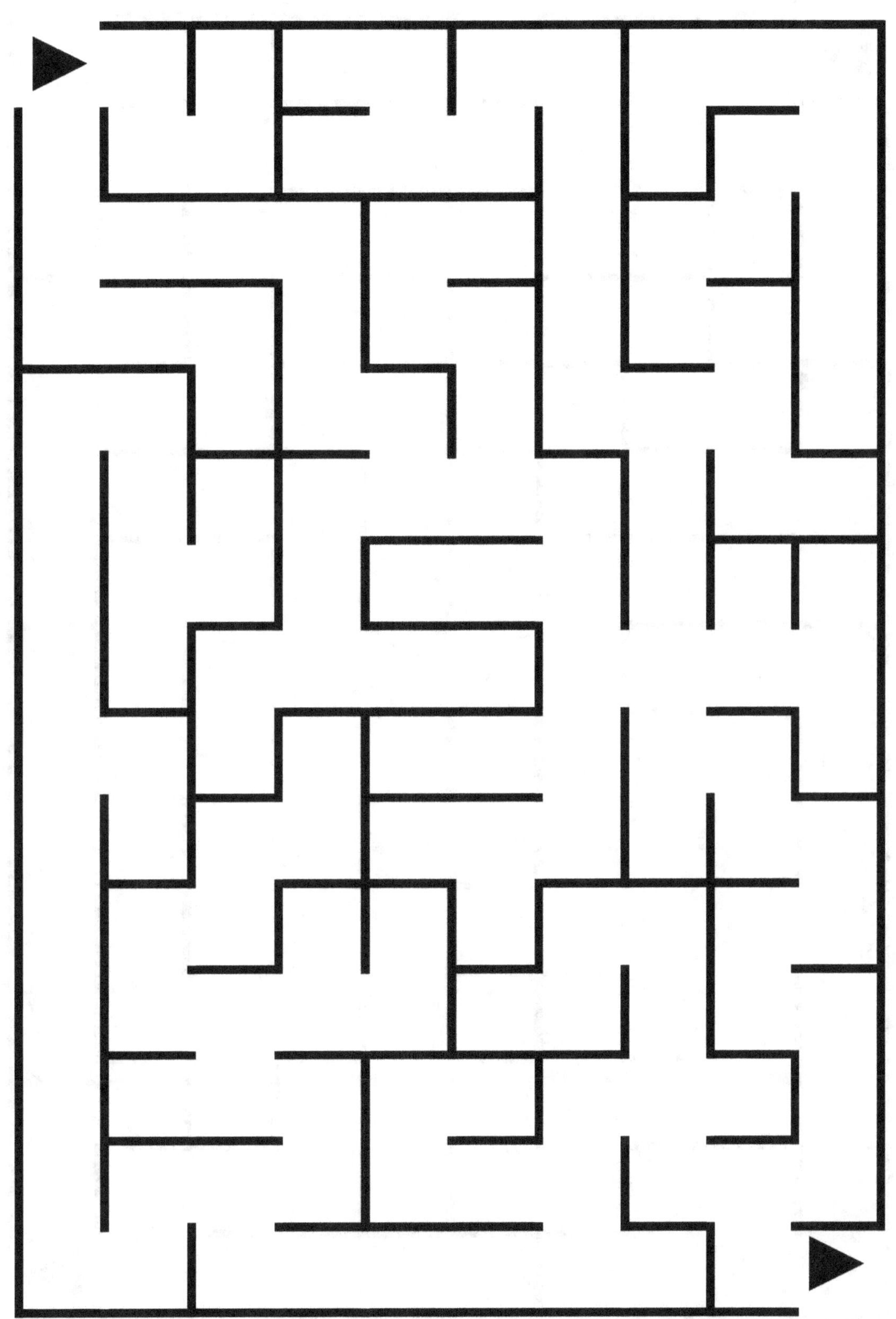

puzzle 19

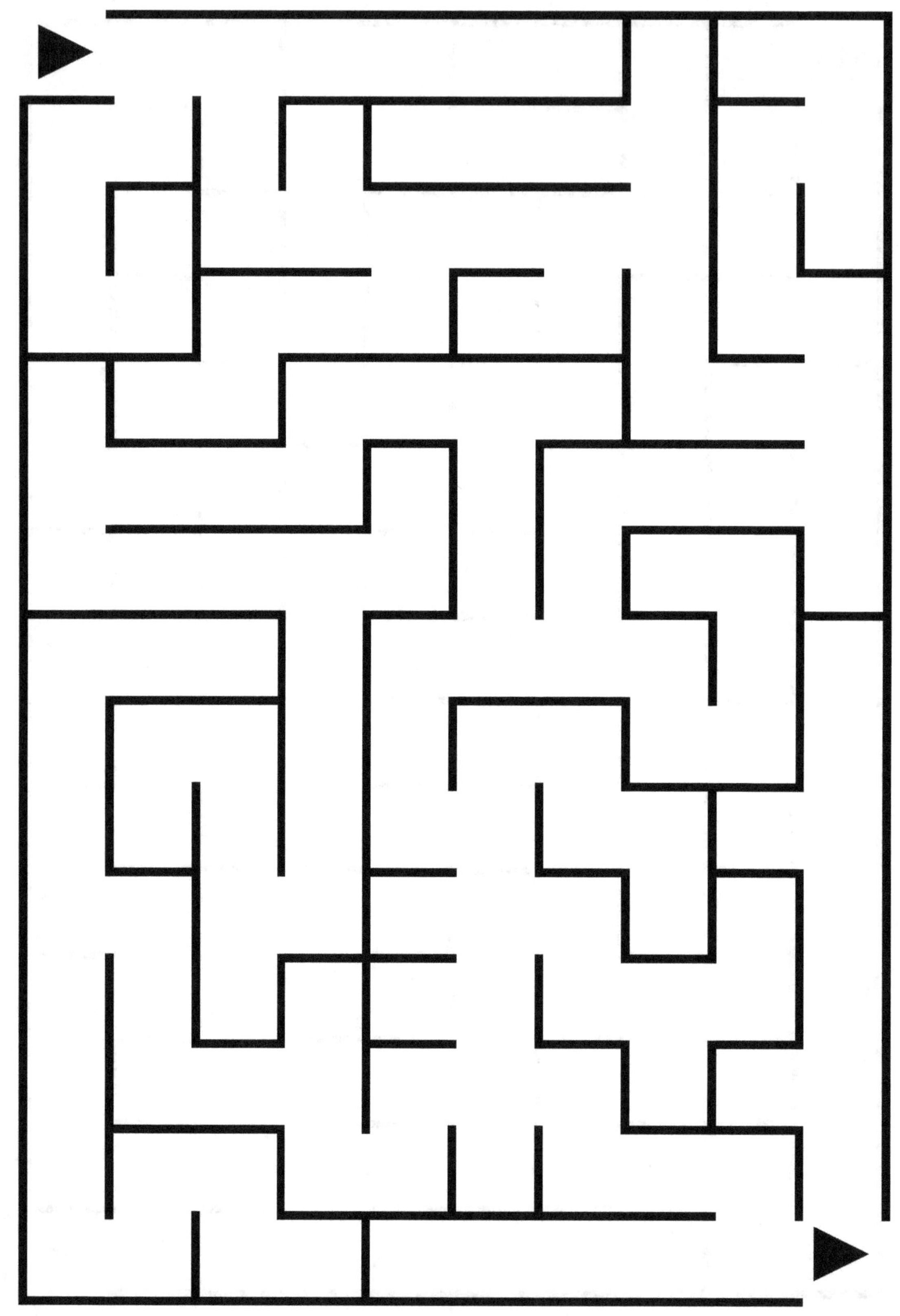

puzzle 20

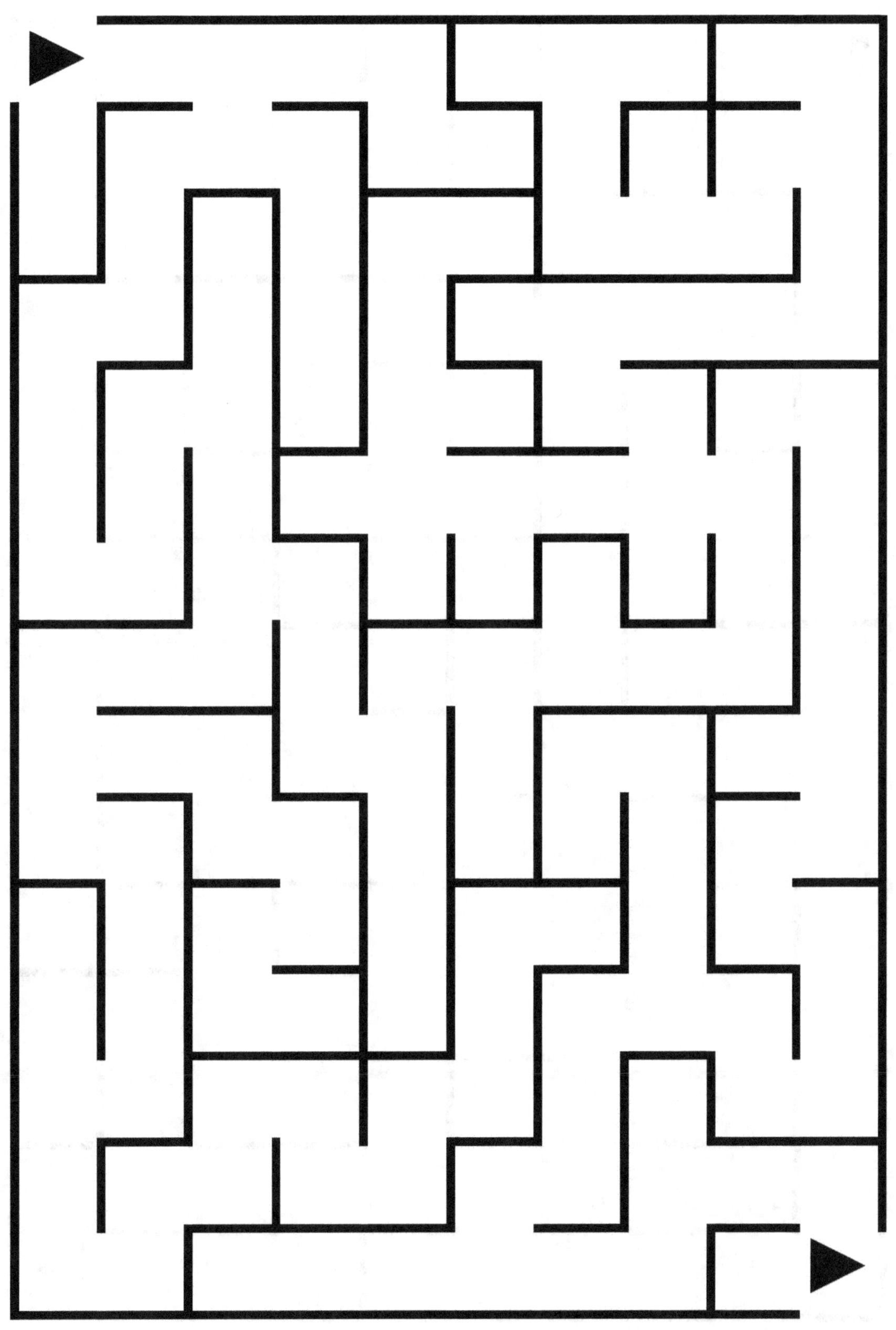

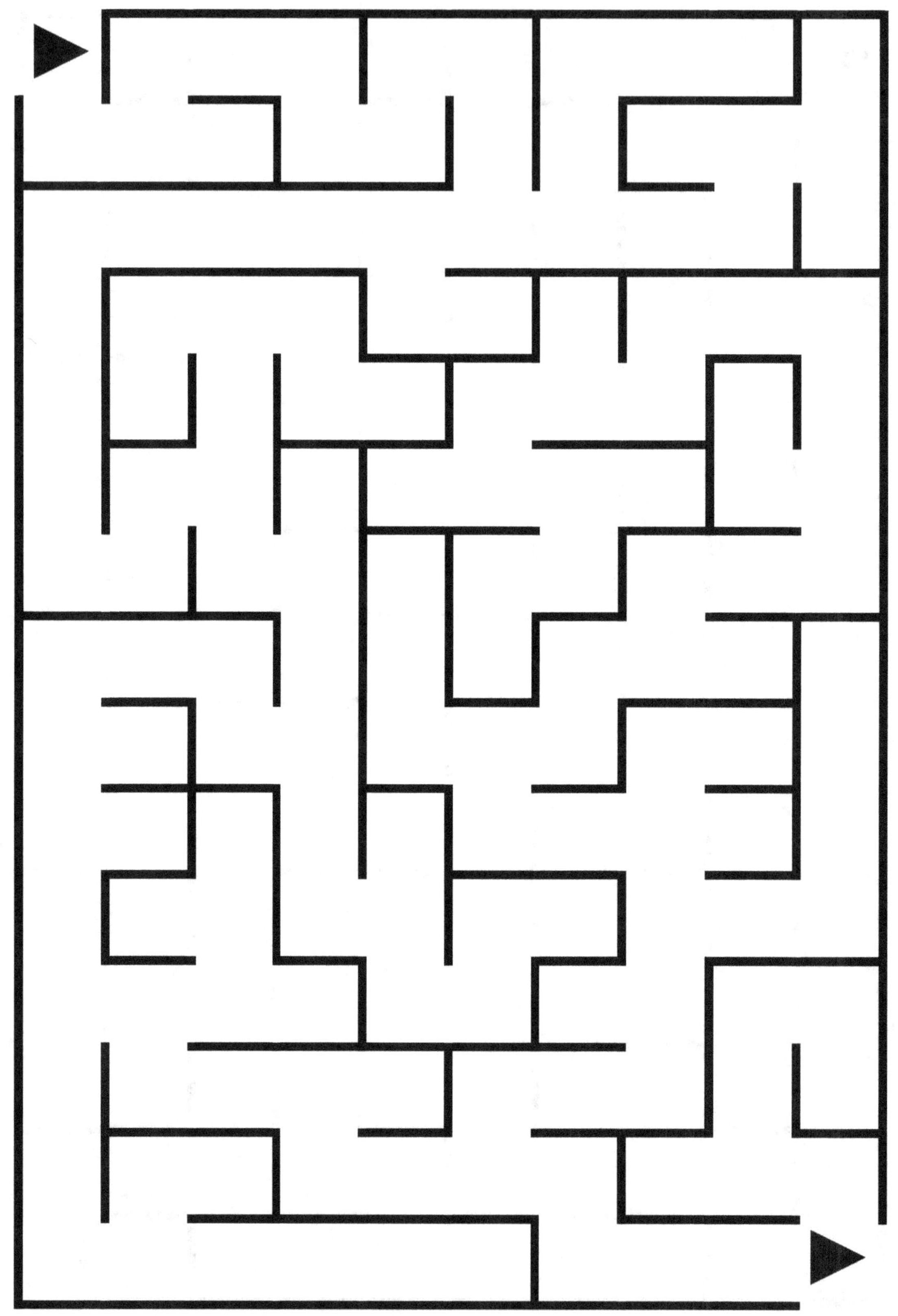

puzzle 22

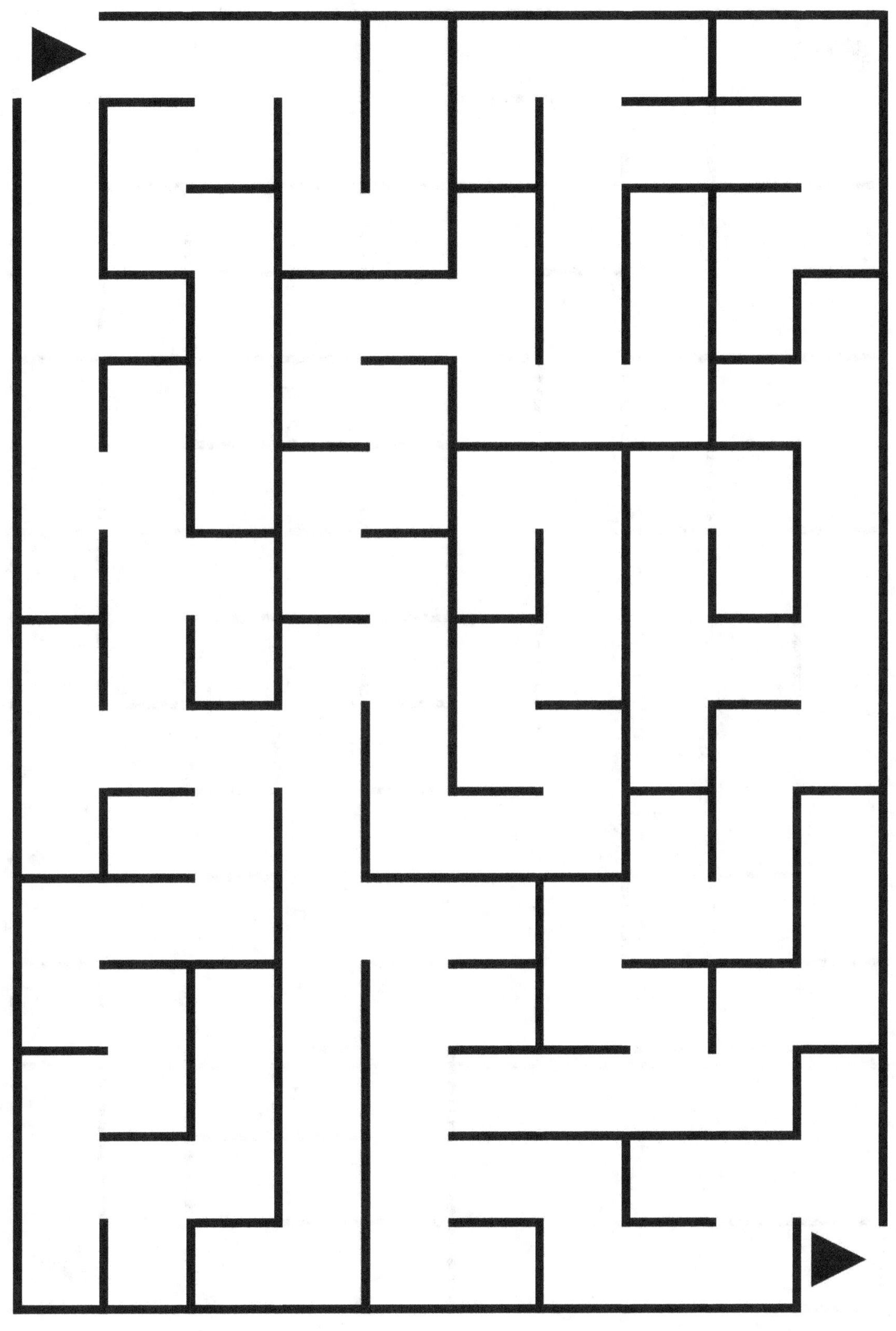

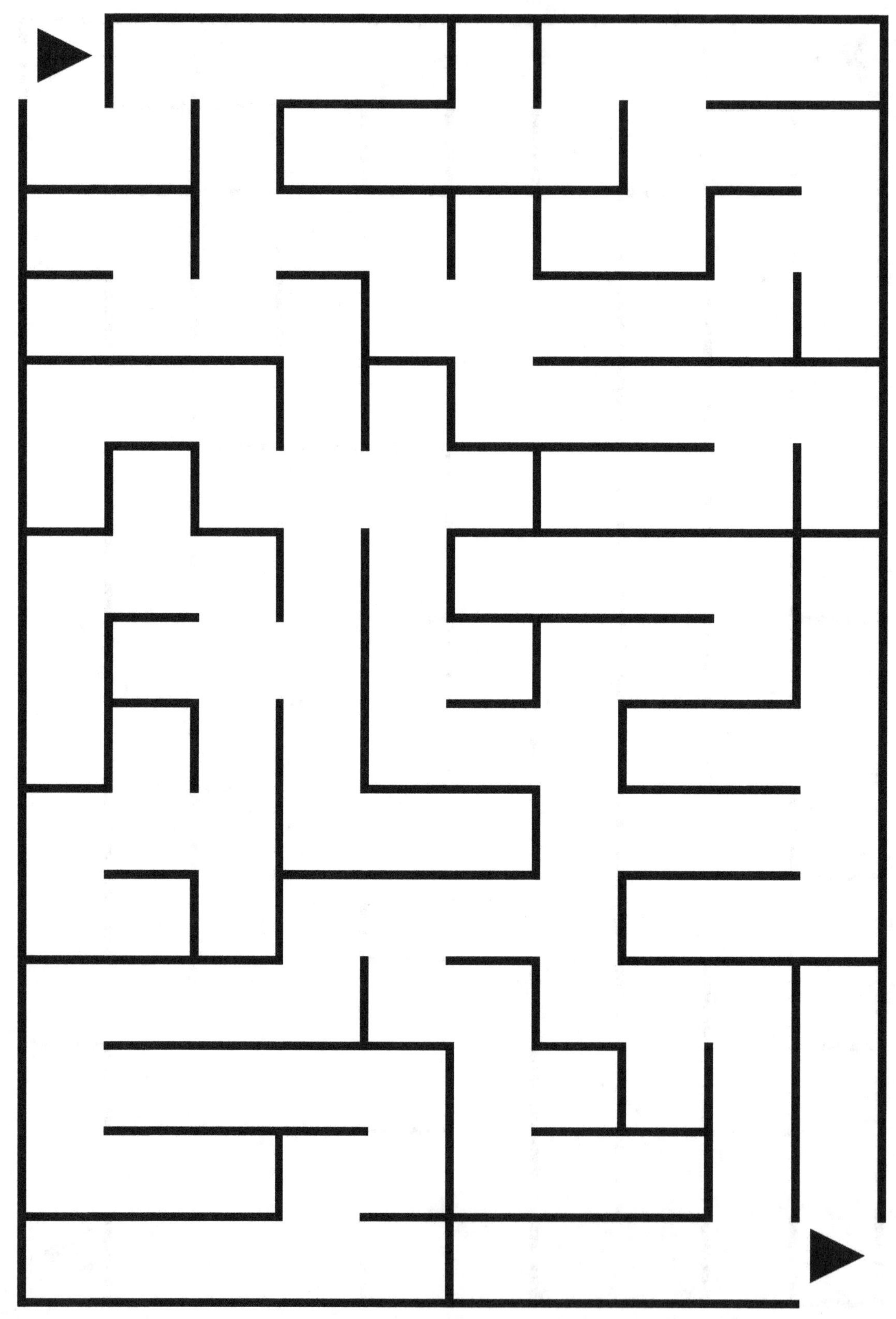

puzzle 24

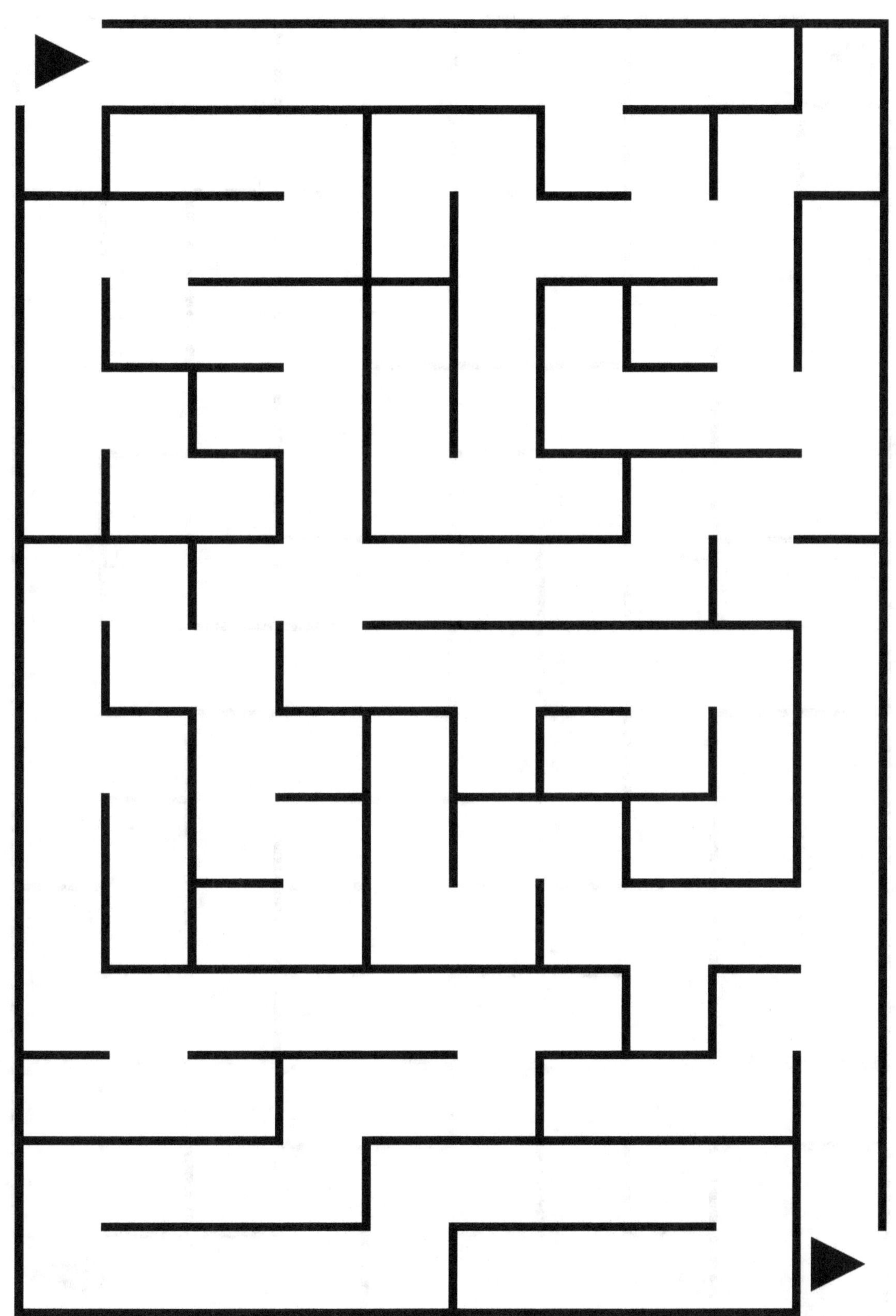

puzzle 25

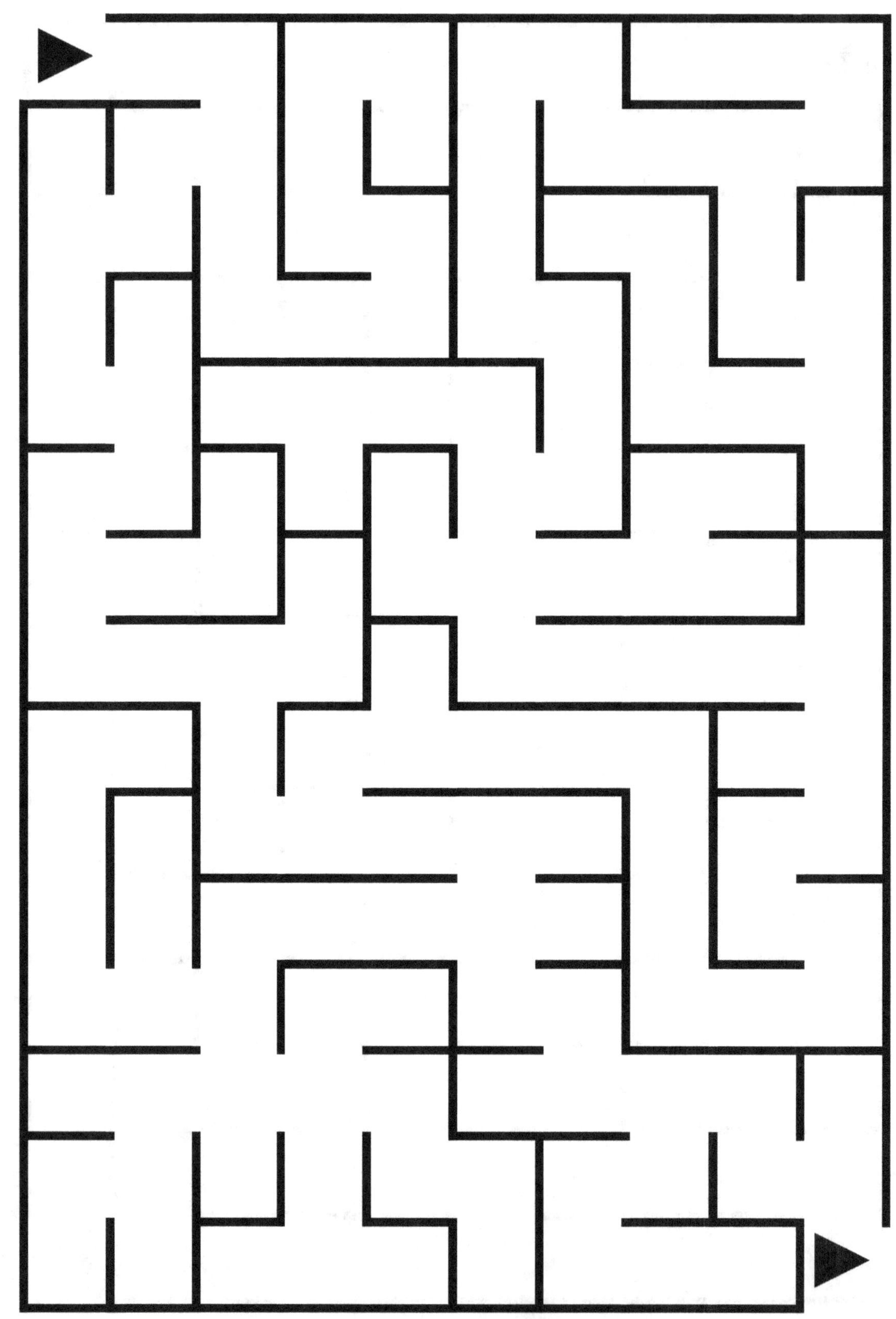

puzzle 26

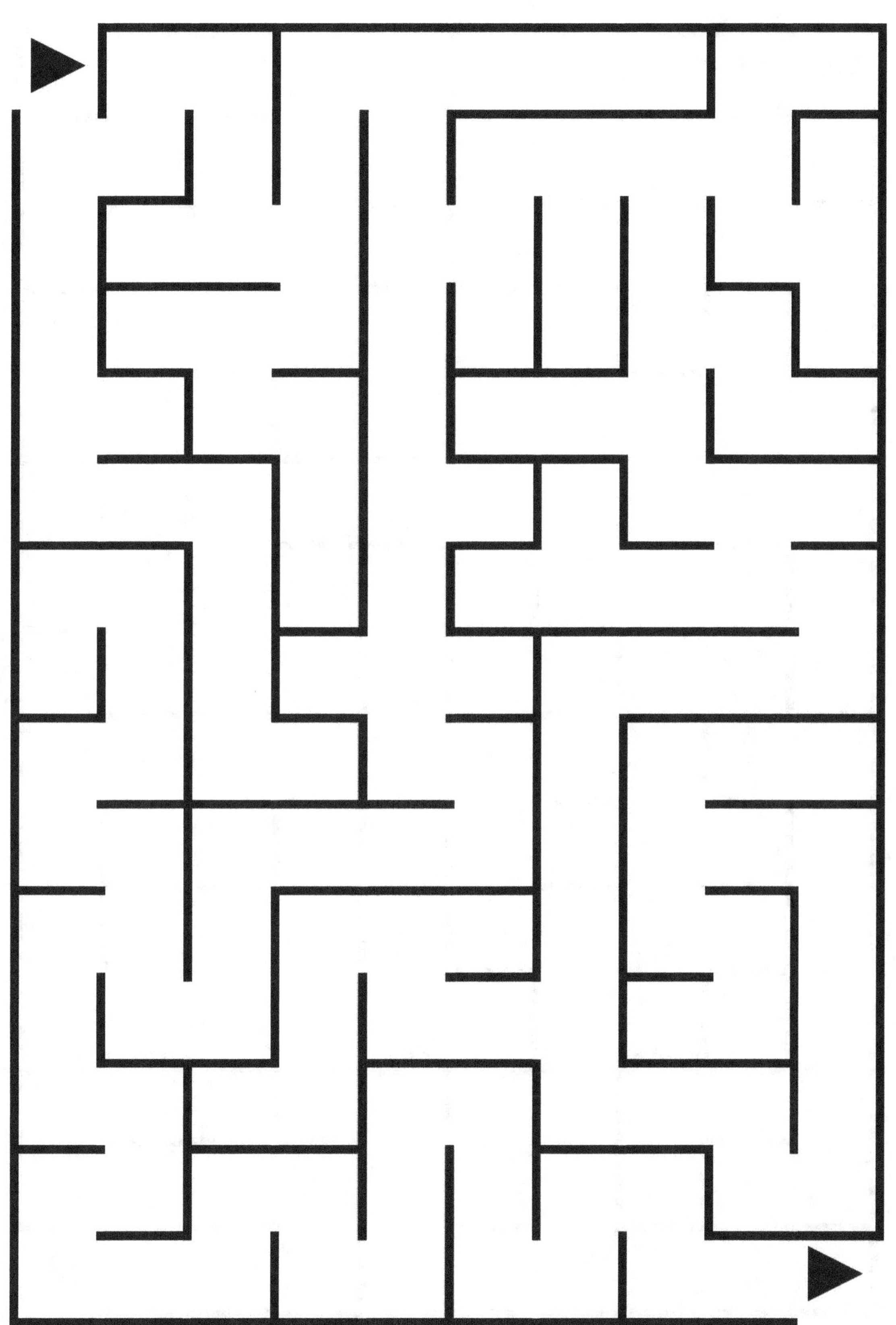

puzzle 27

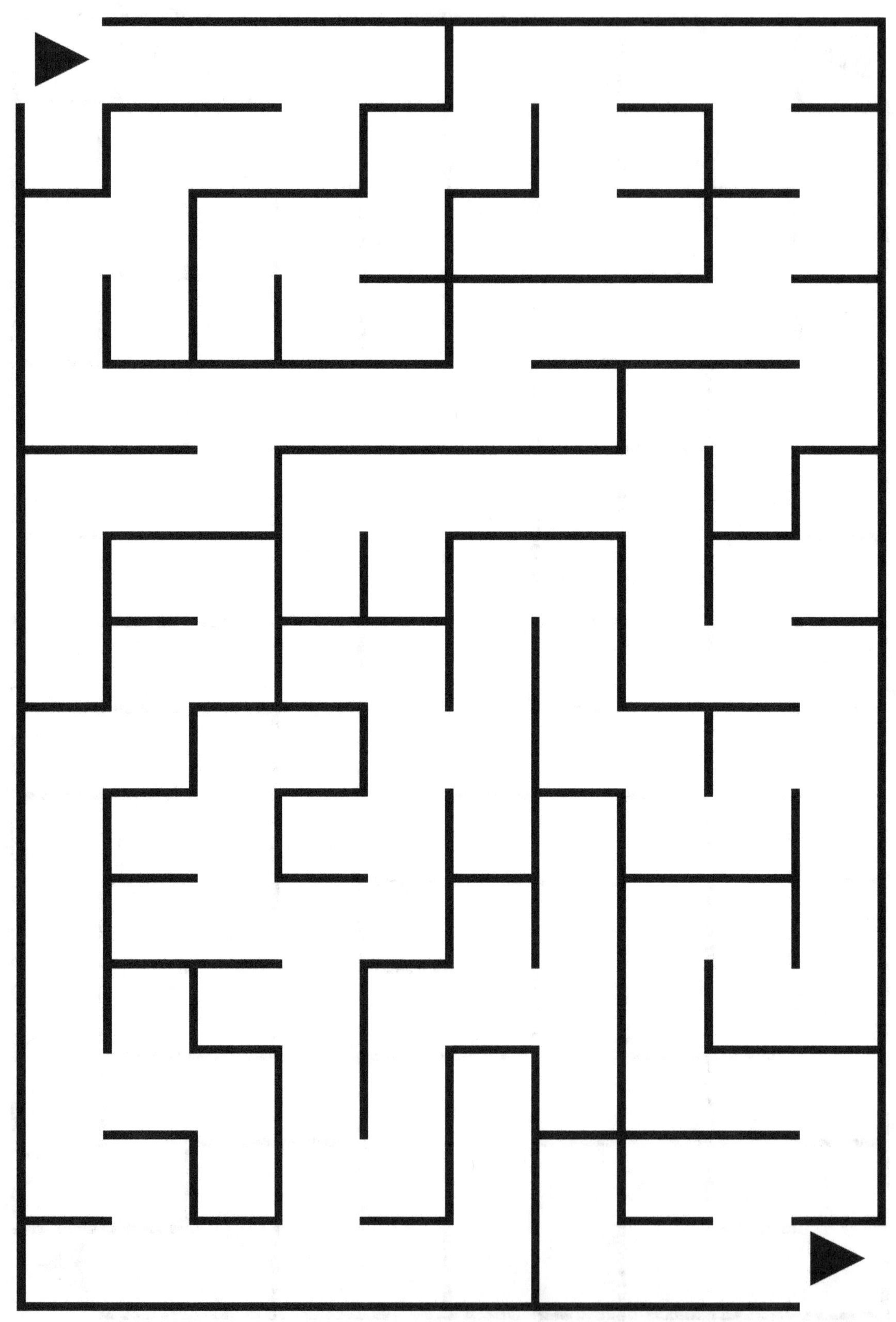

puzzle 28

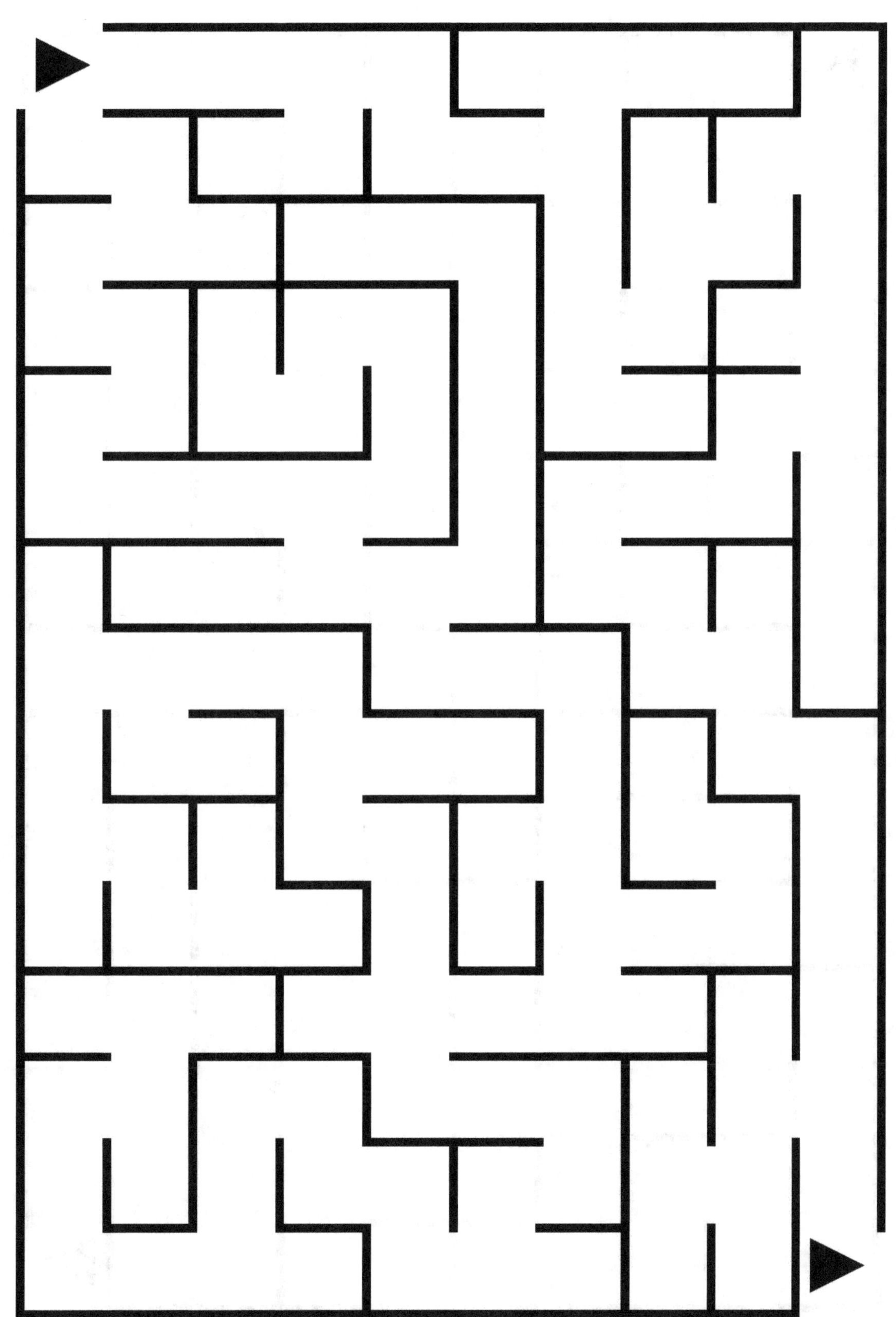

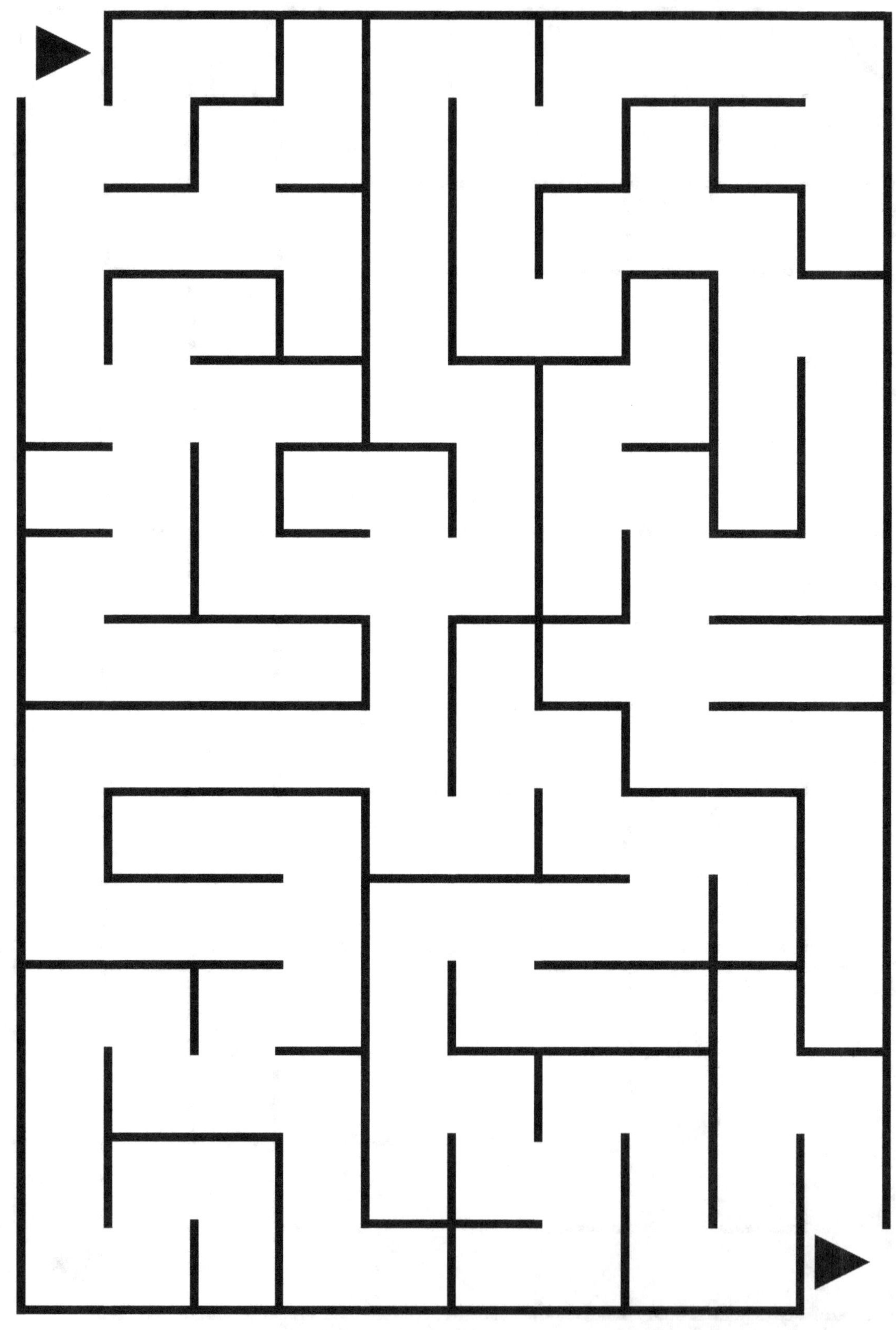

puzzle 30

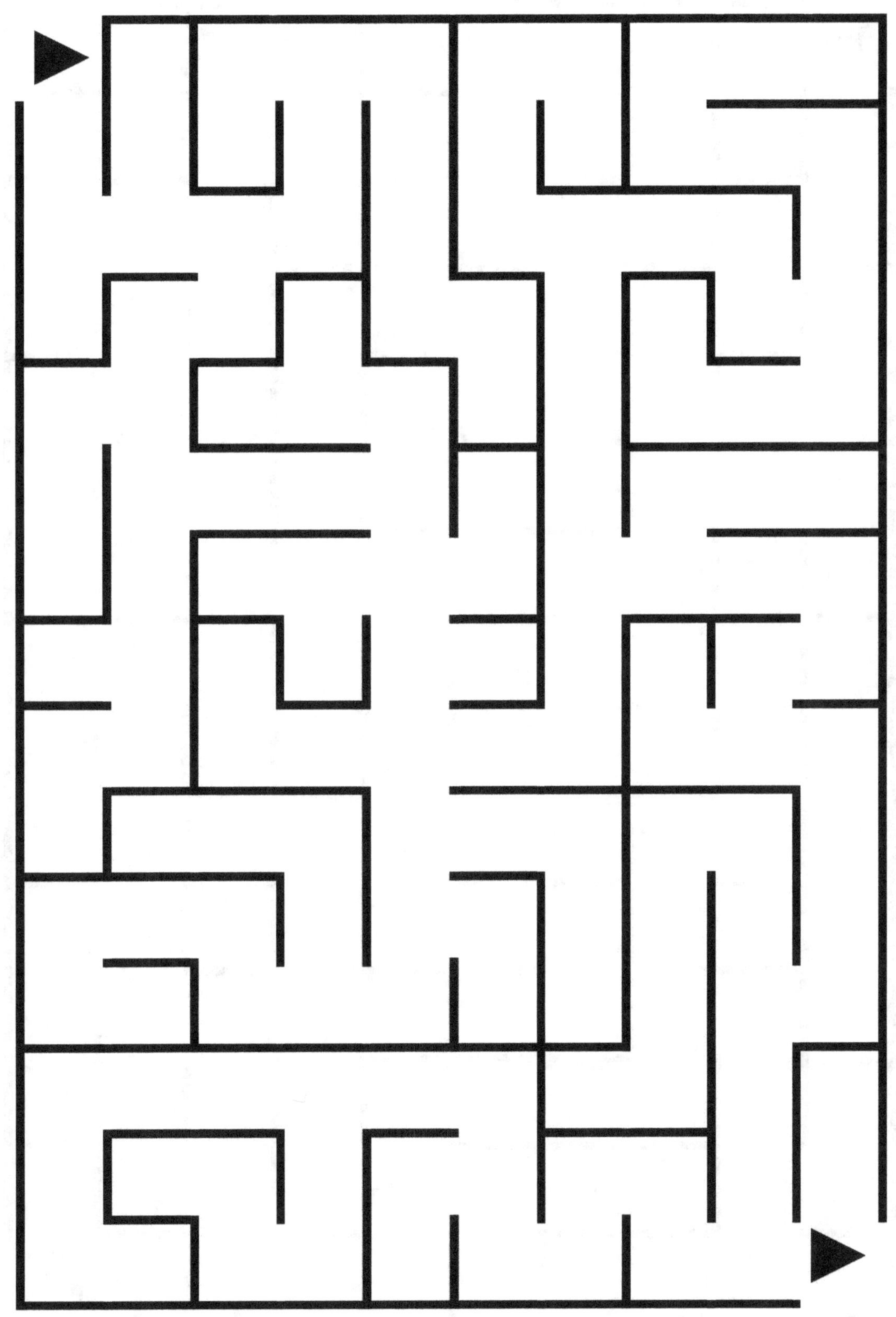

puzzle 31

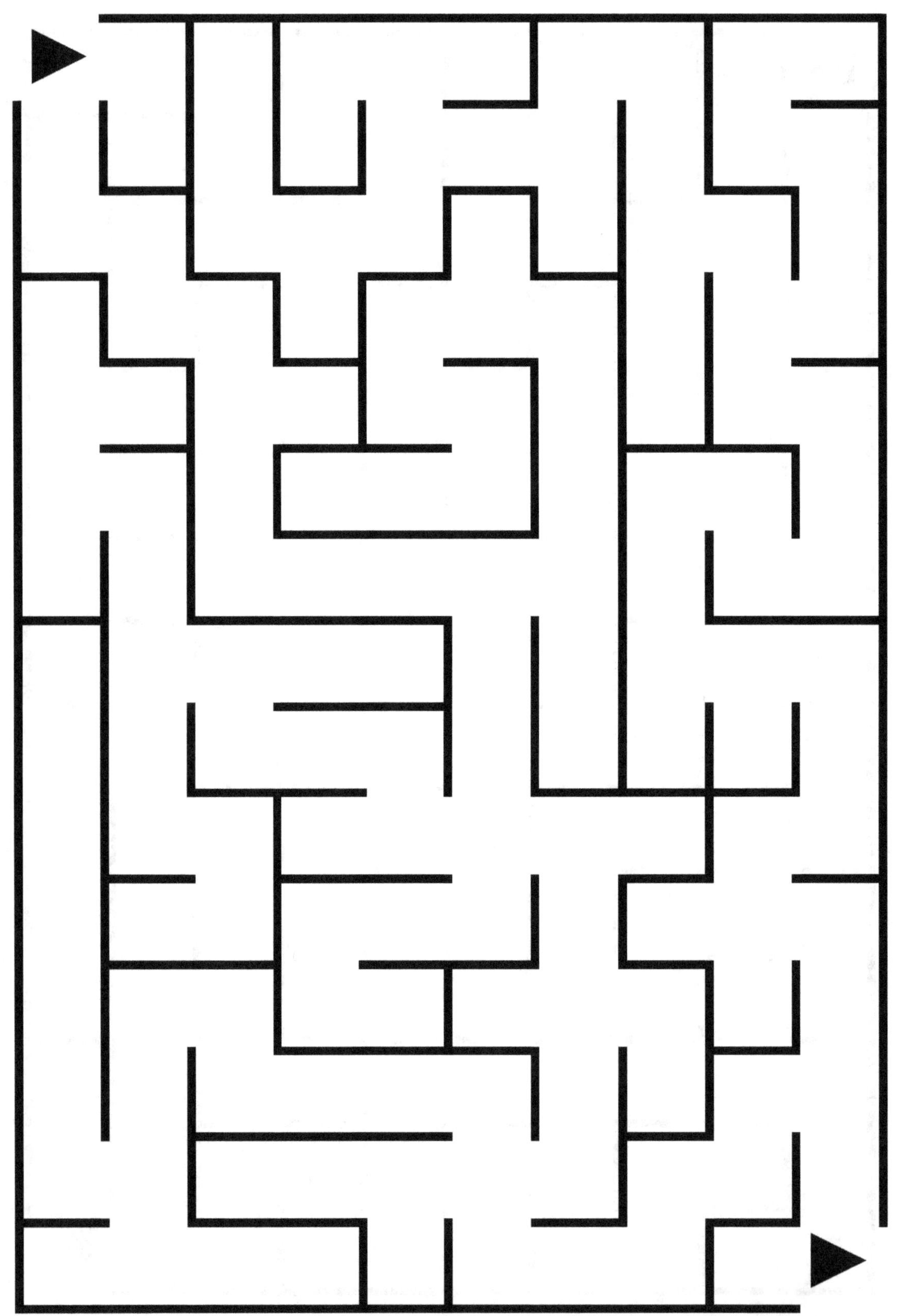

puzzle 32

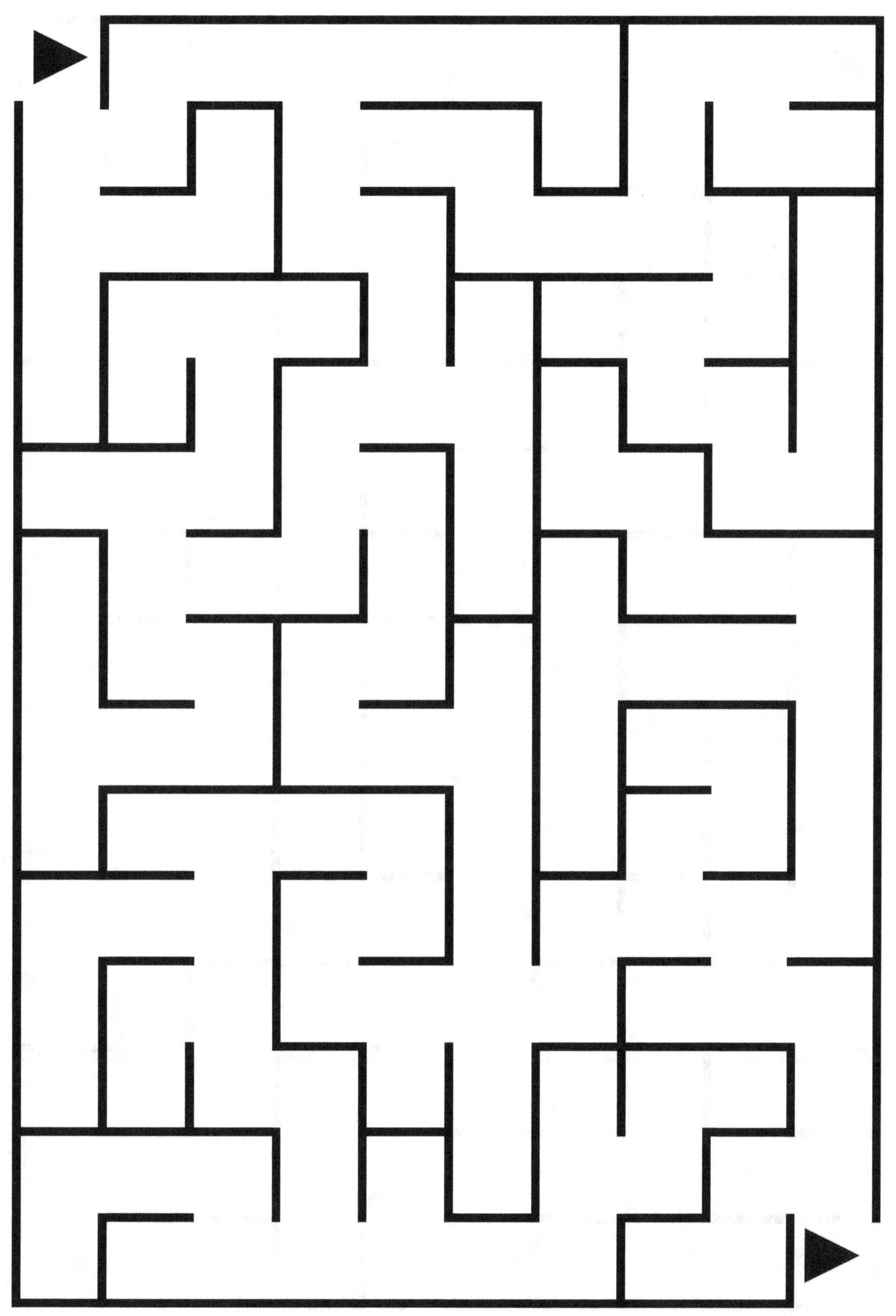

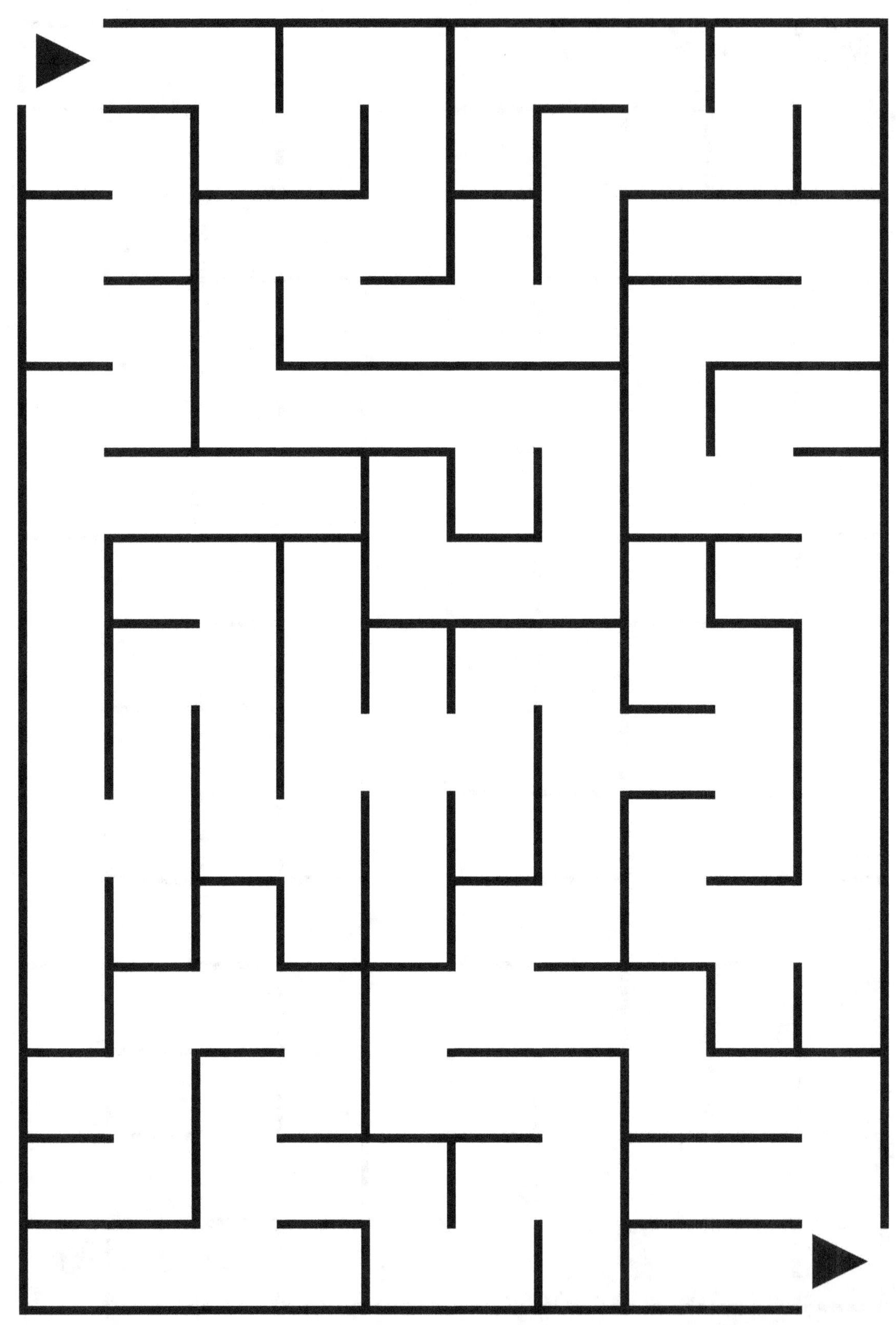

puzzle 34

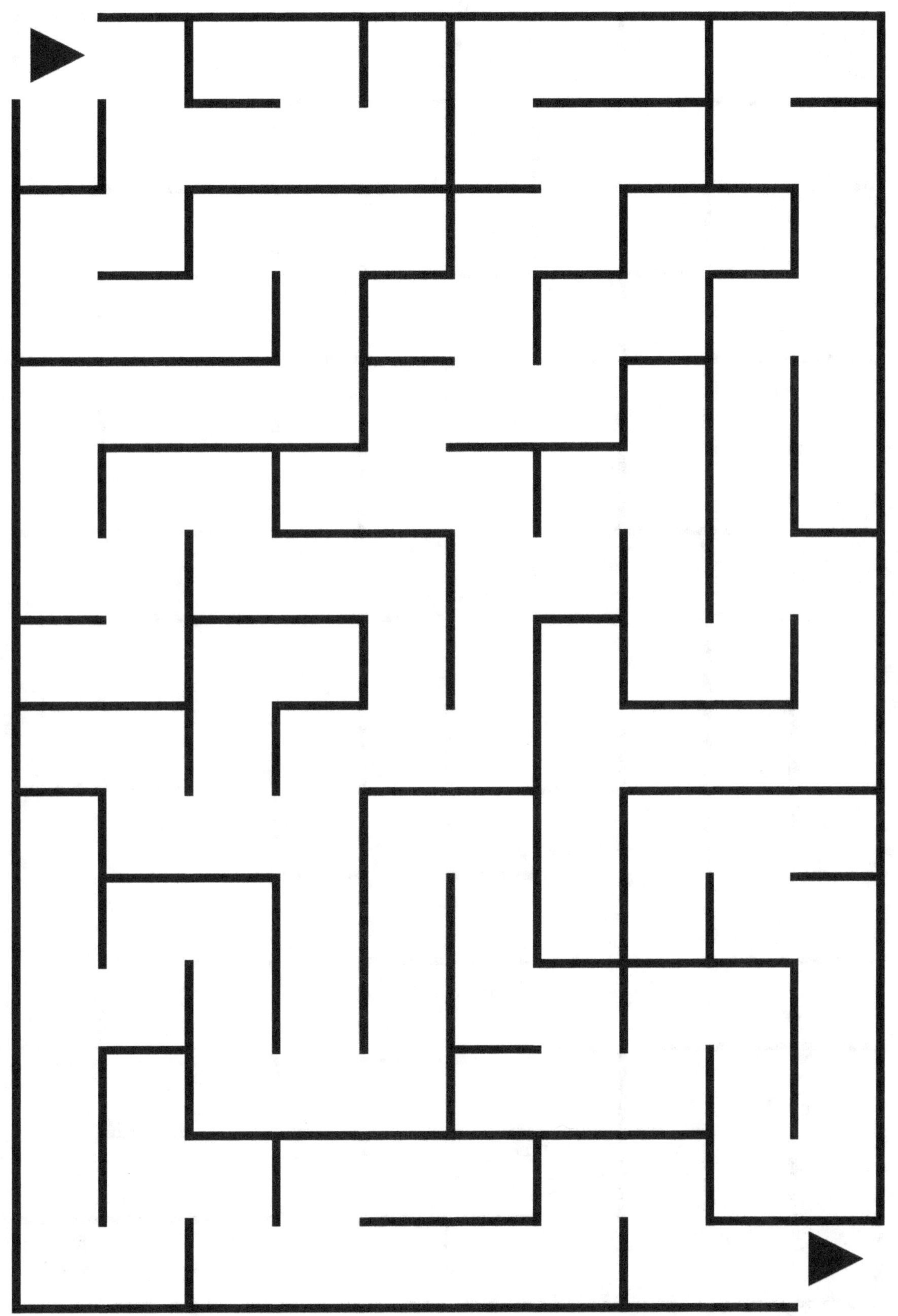

puzzle 35

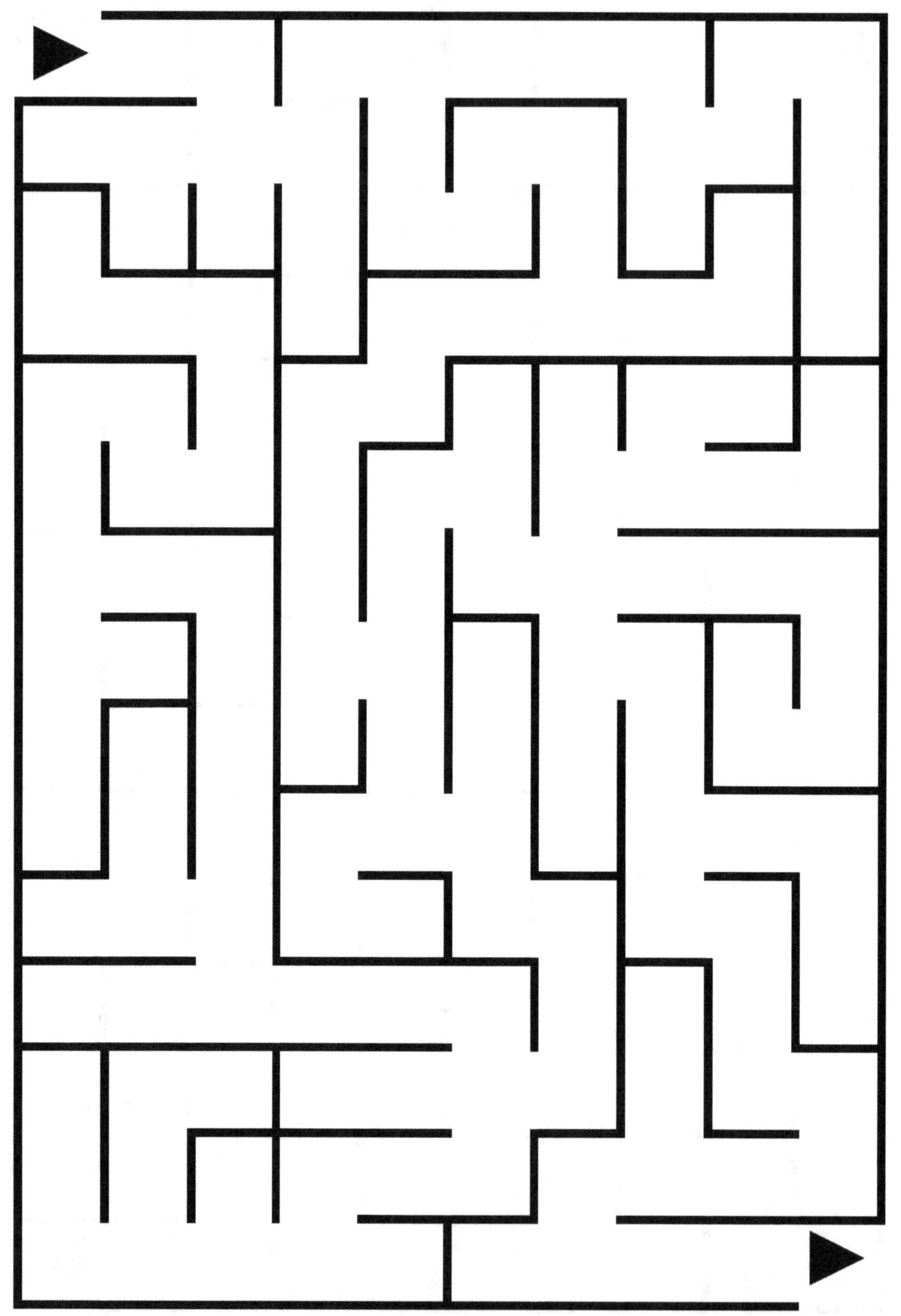

puzzle 36

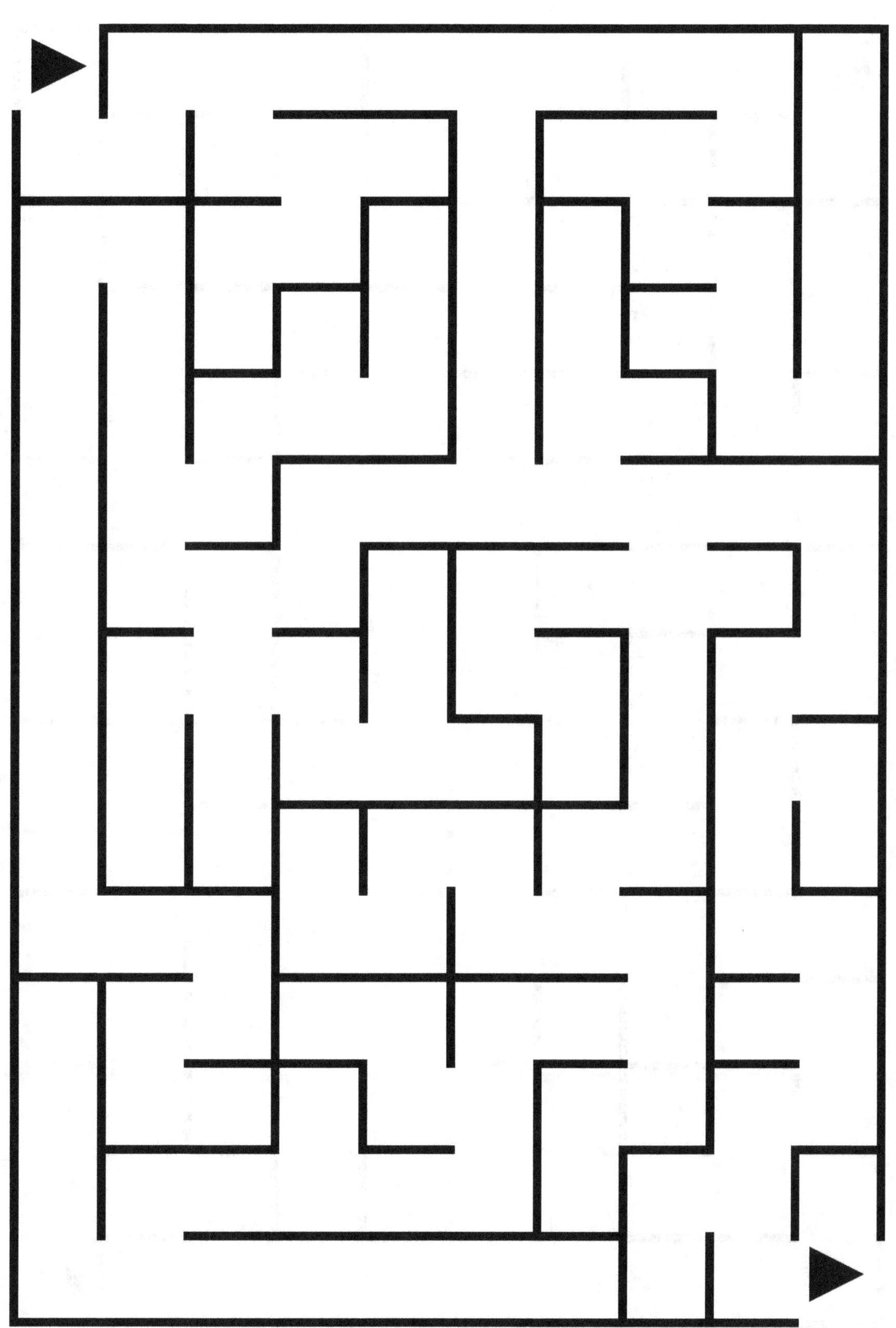

puzzle 37

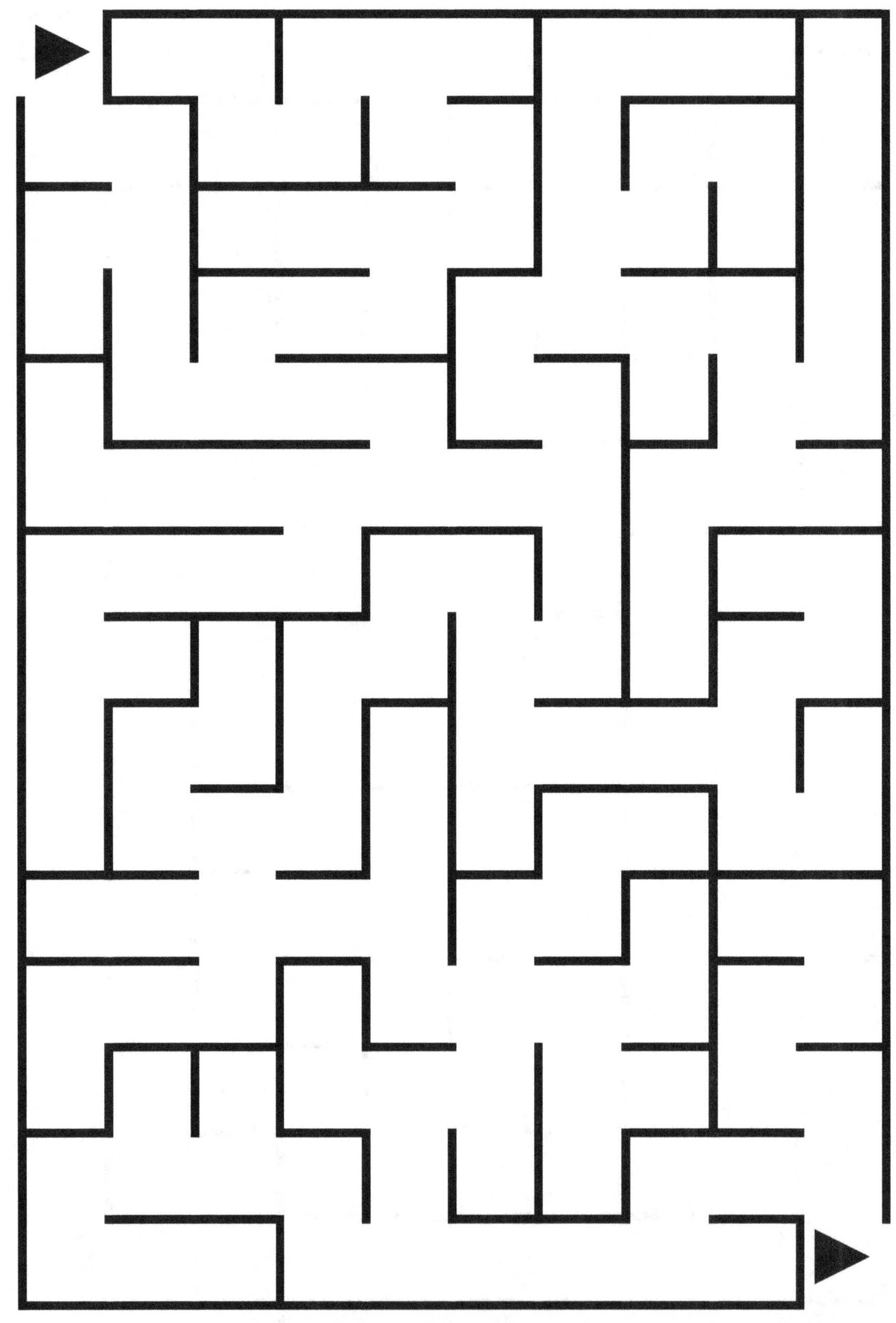

puzzle 38

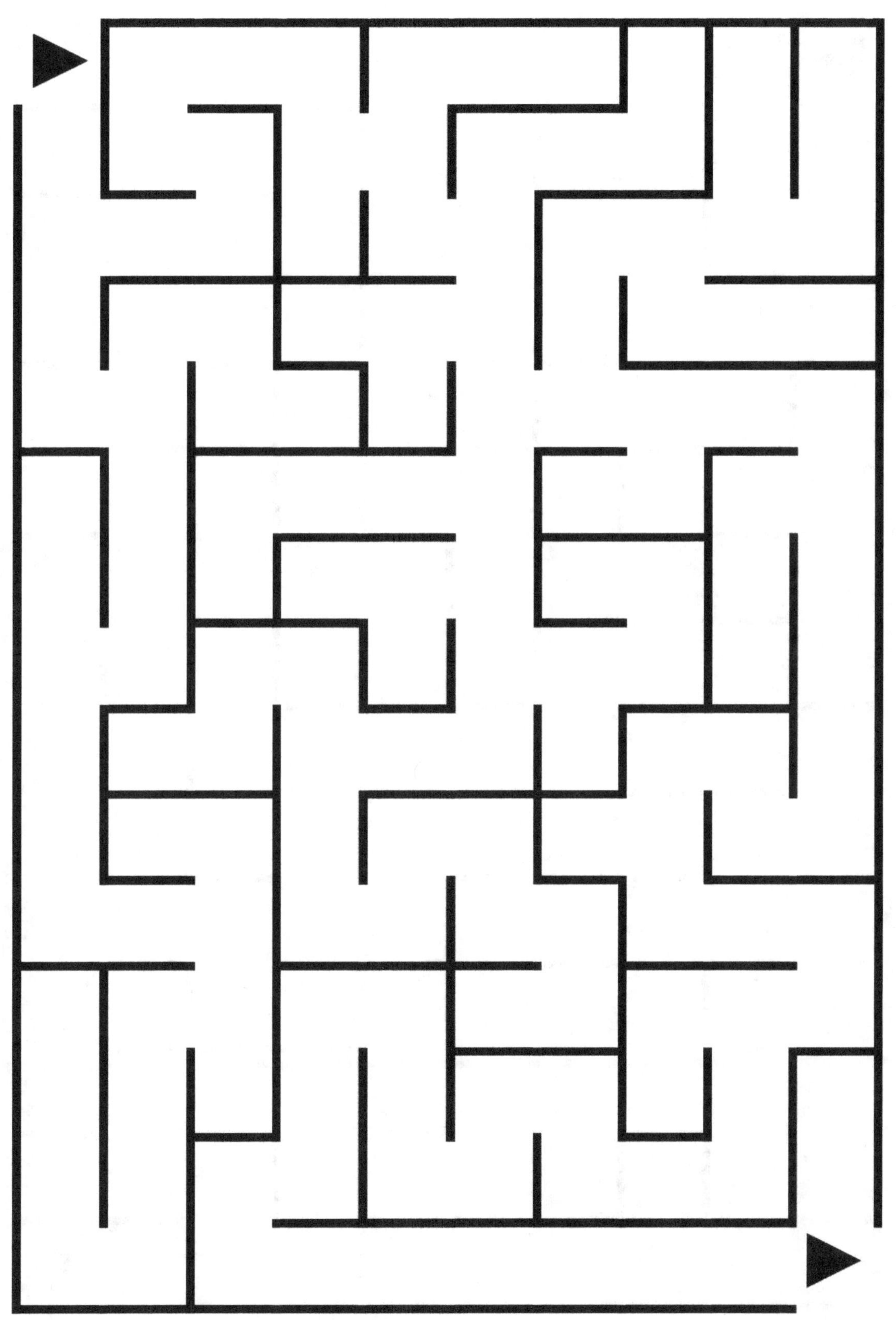

puzzle 39

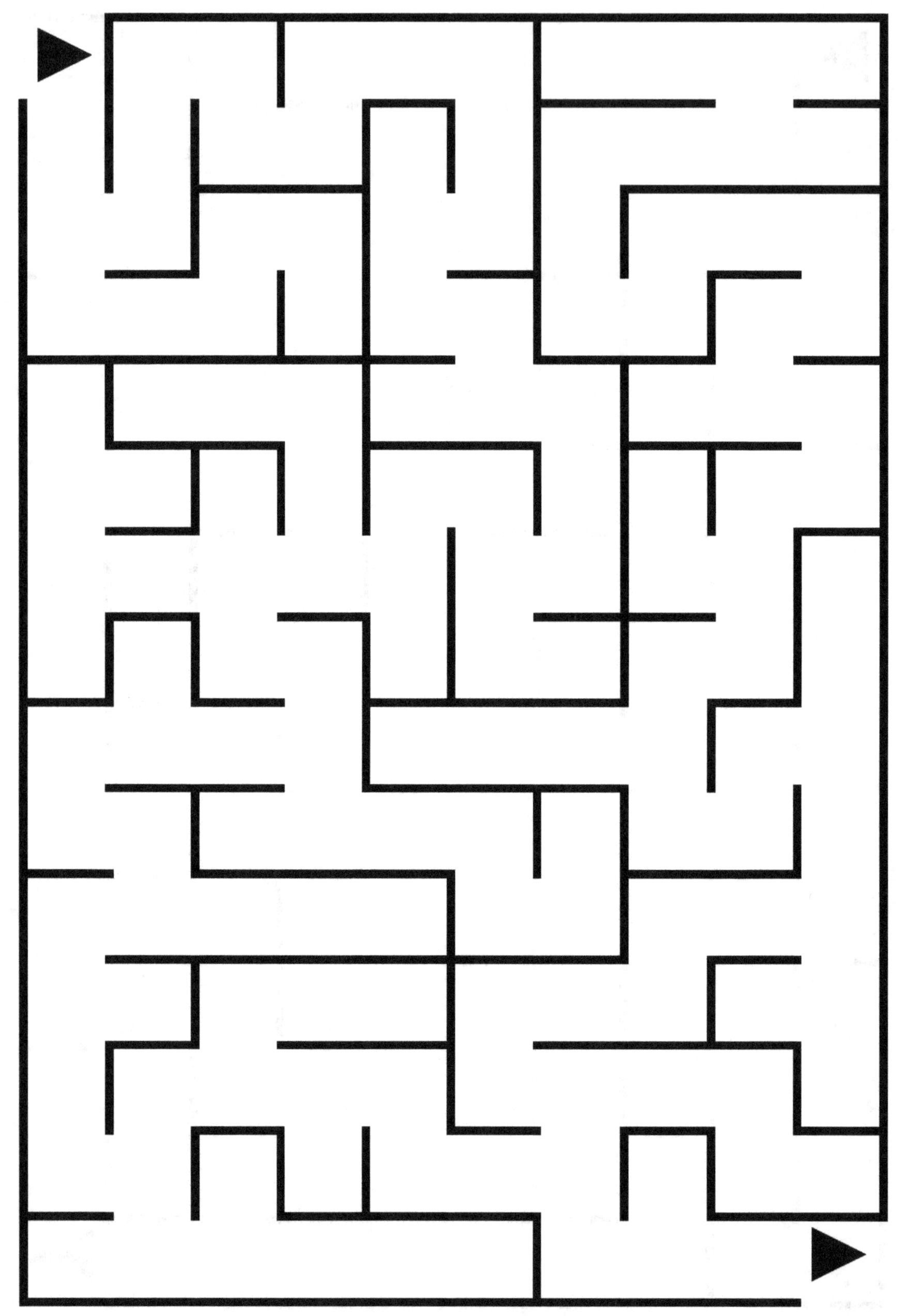

puzzle 40

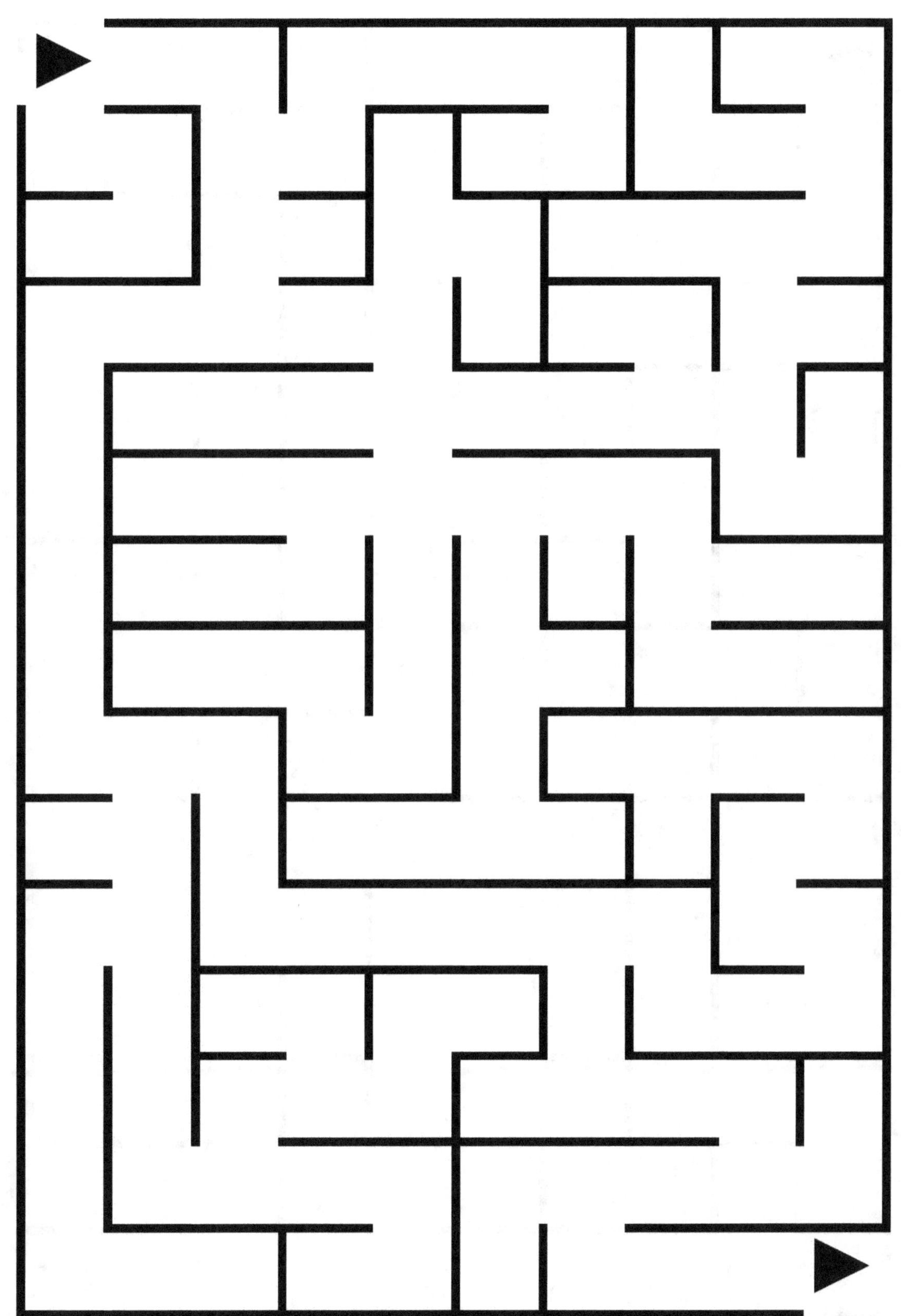

puzzle 41

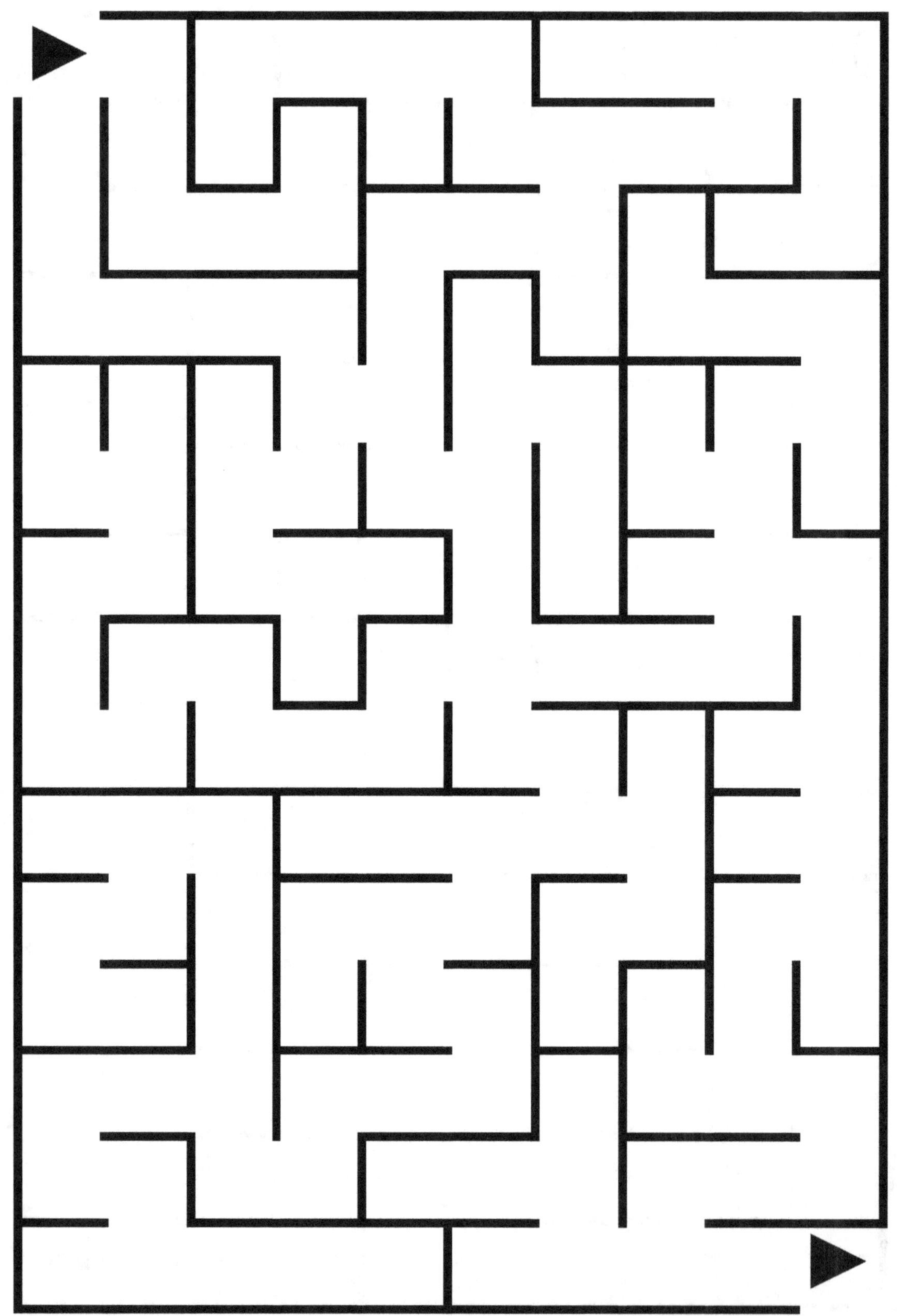

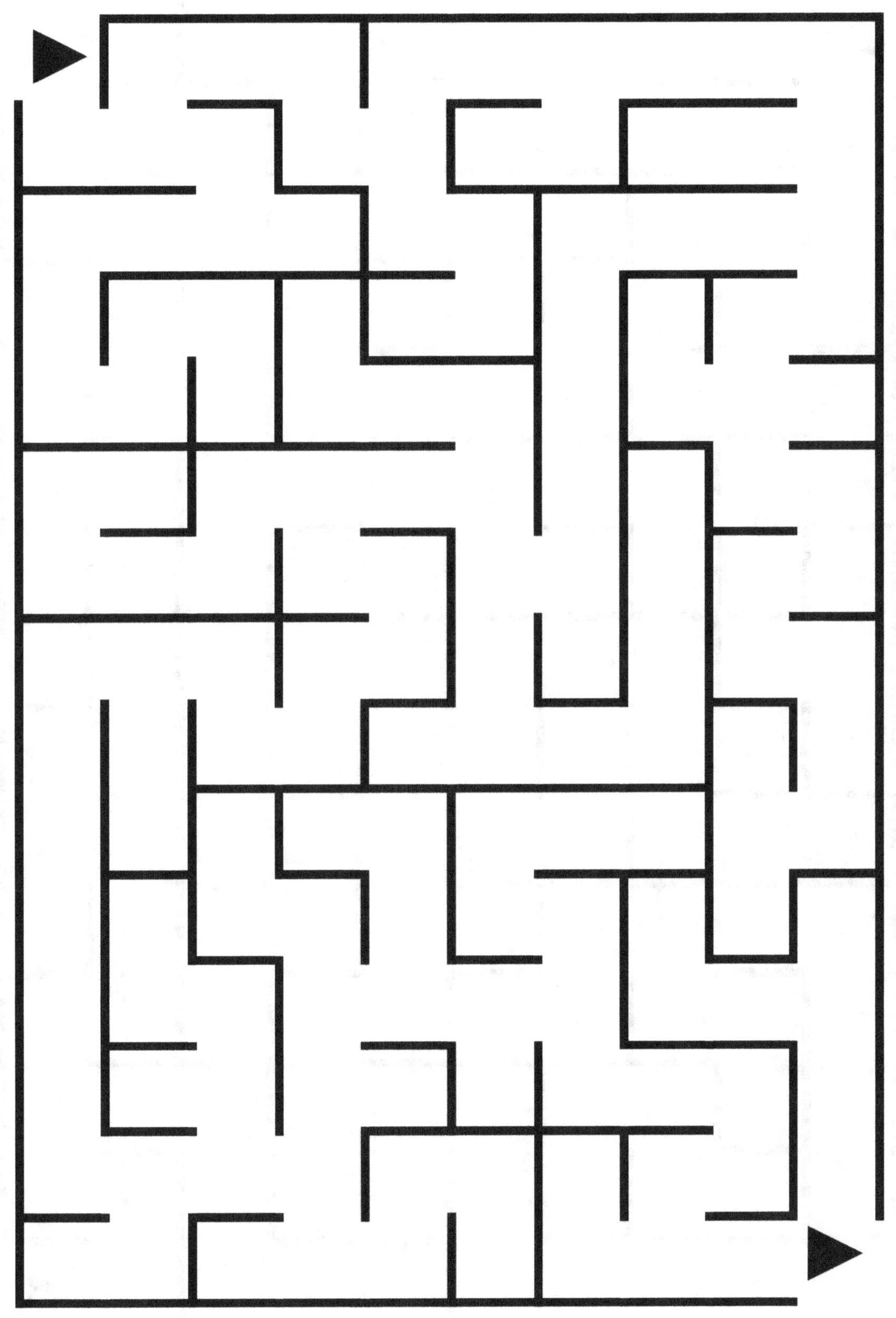

puzzle 43

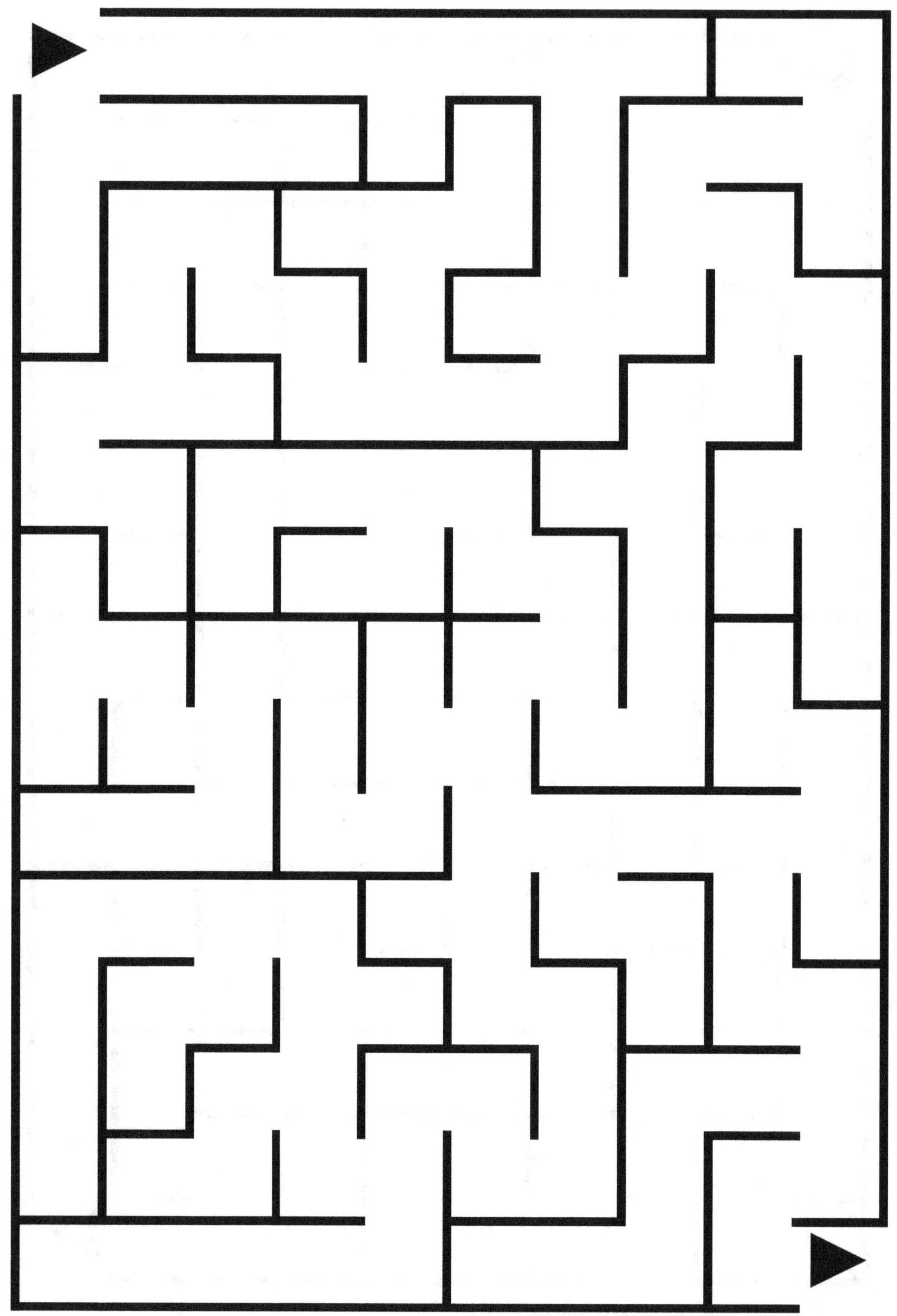

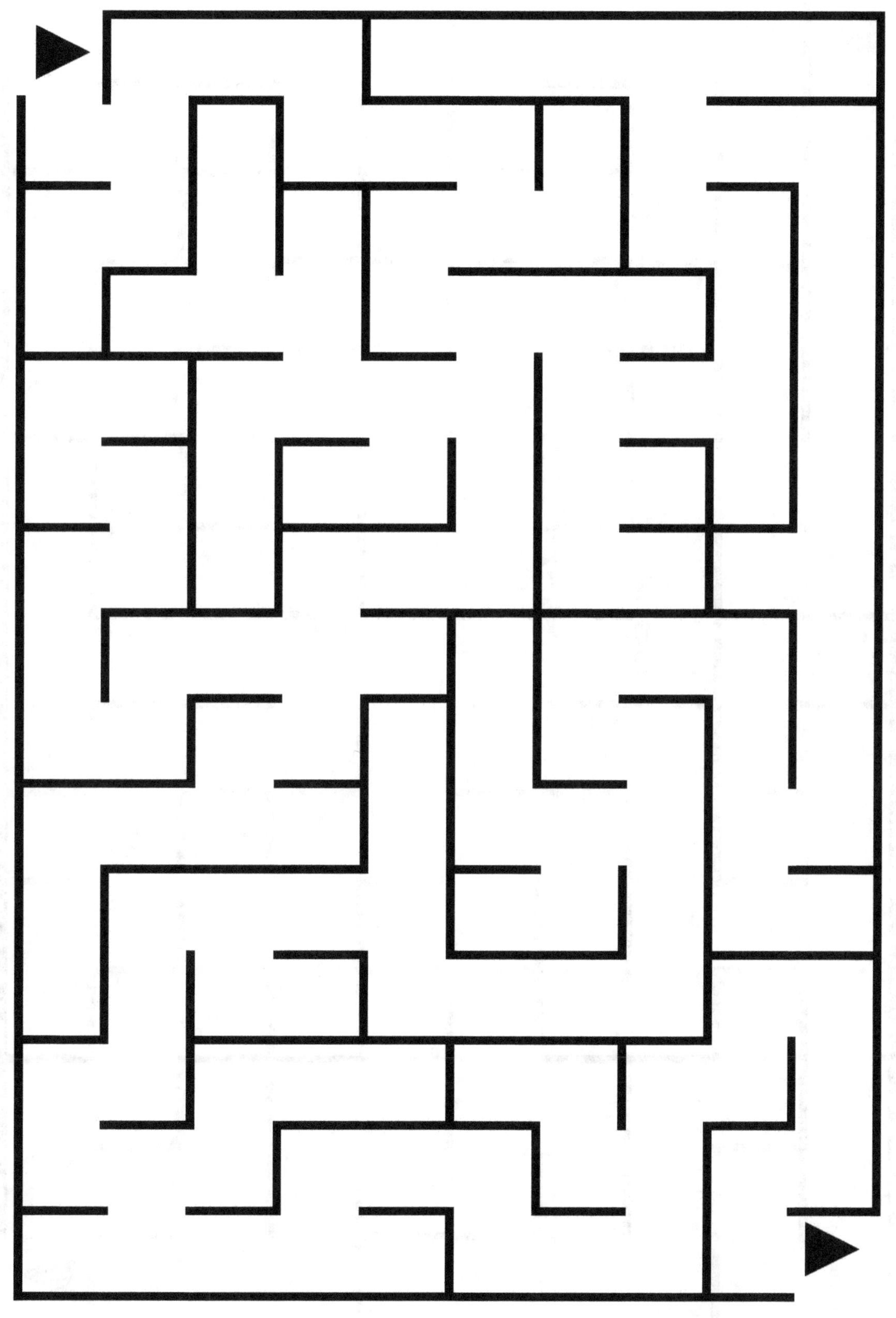

puzzle 45

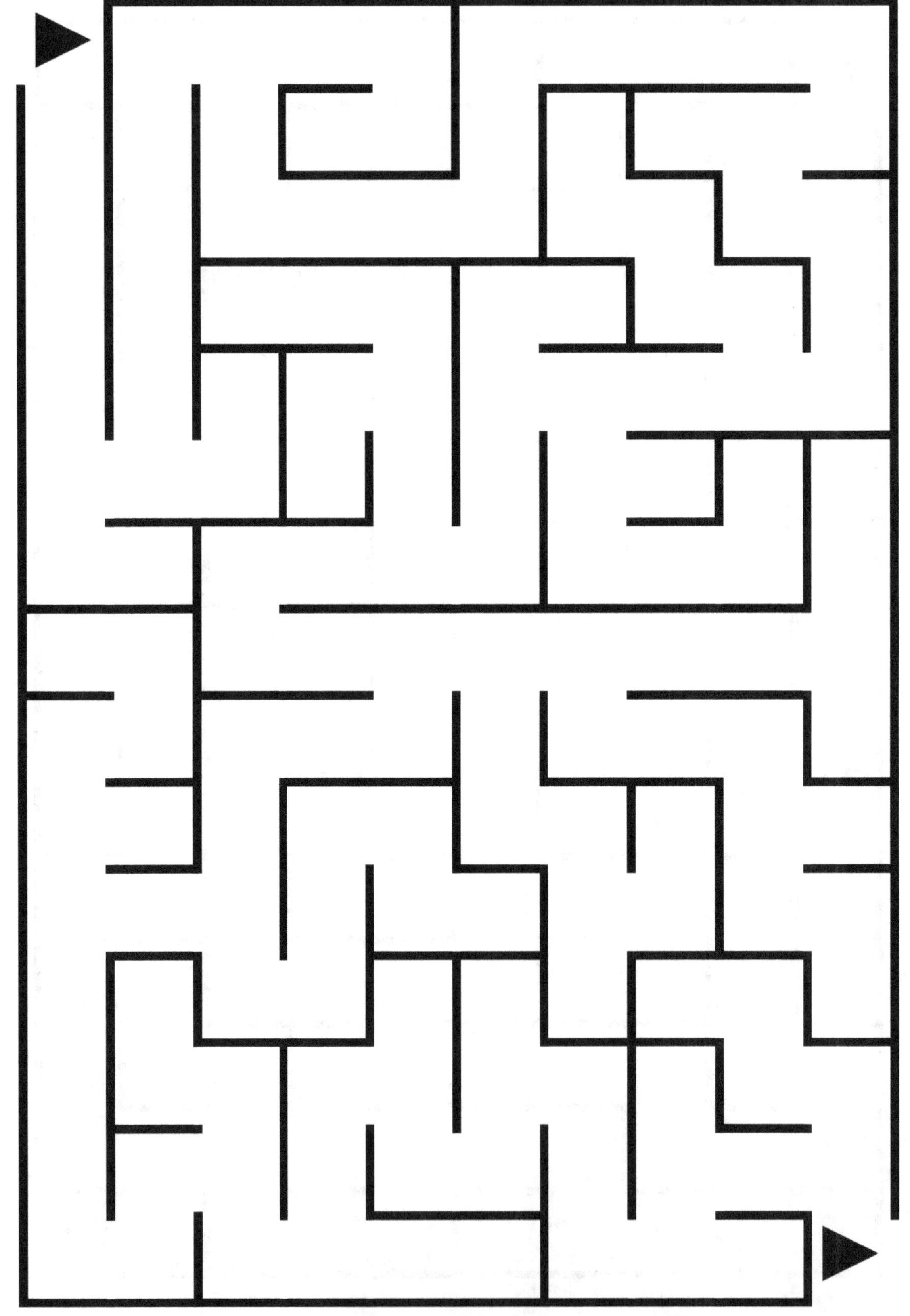

puzzle 46

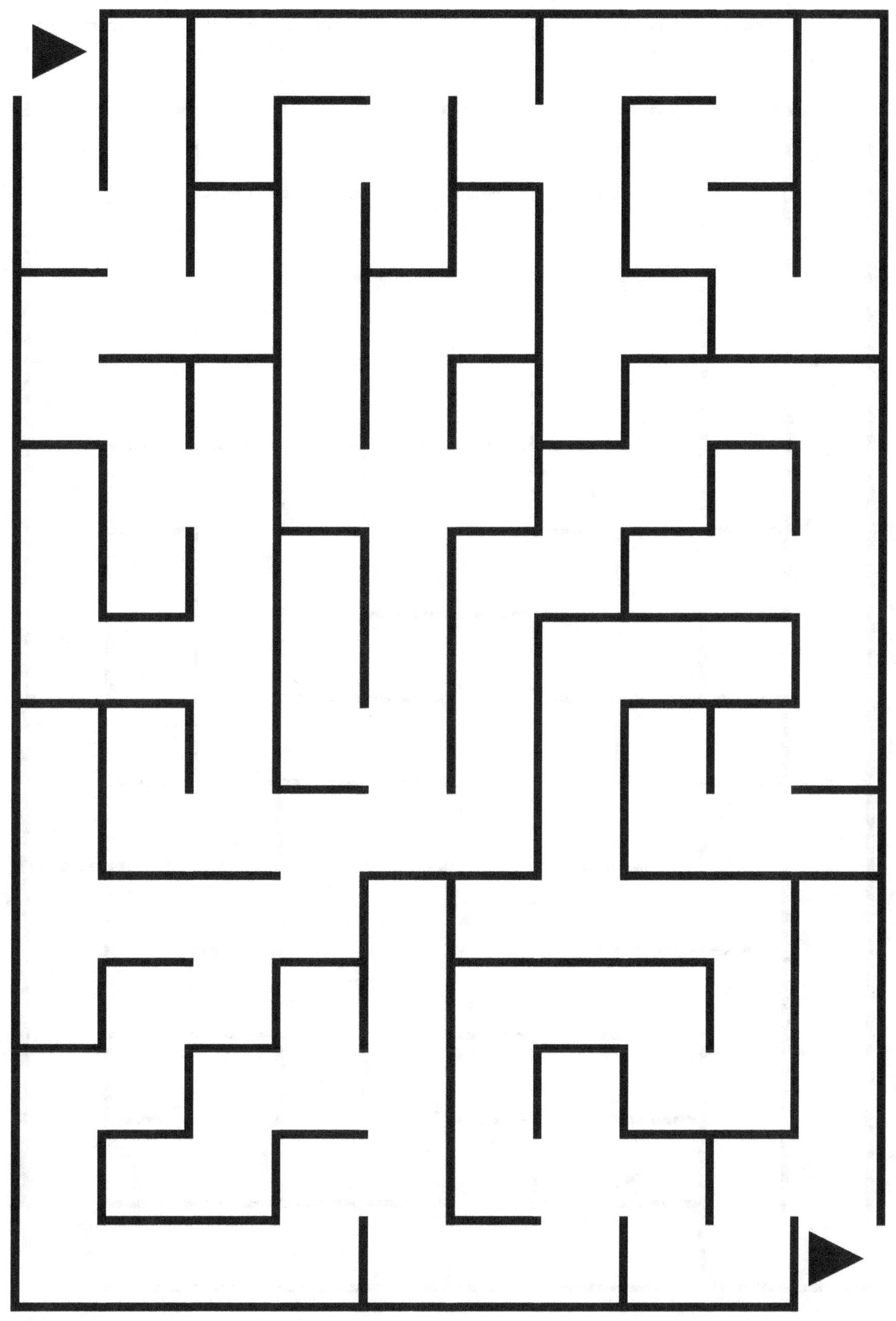

puzzle 47

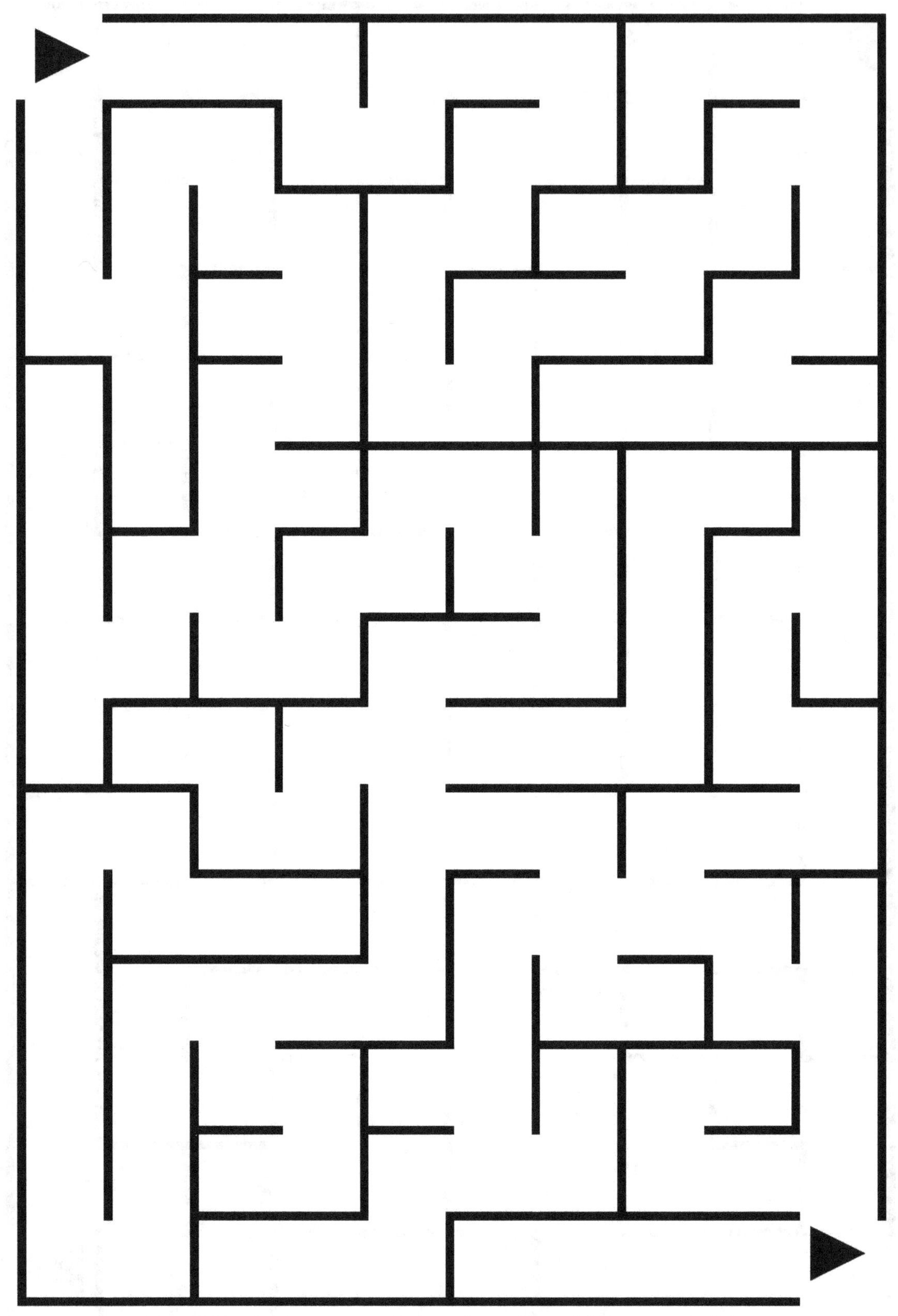

puzzle 48

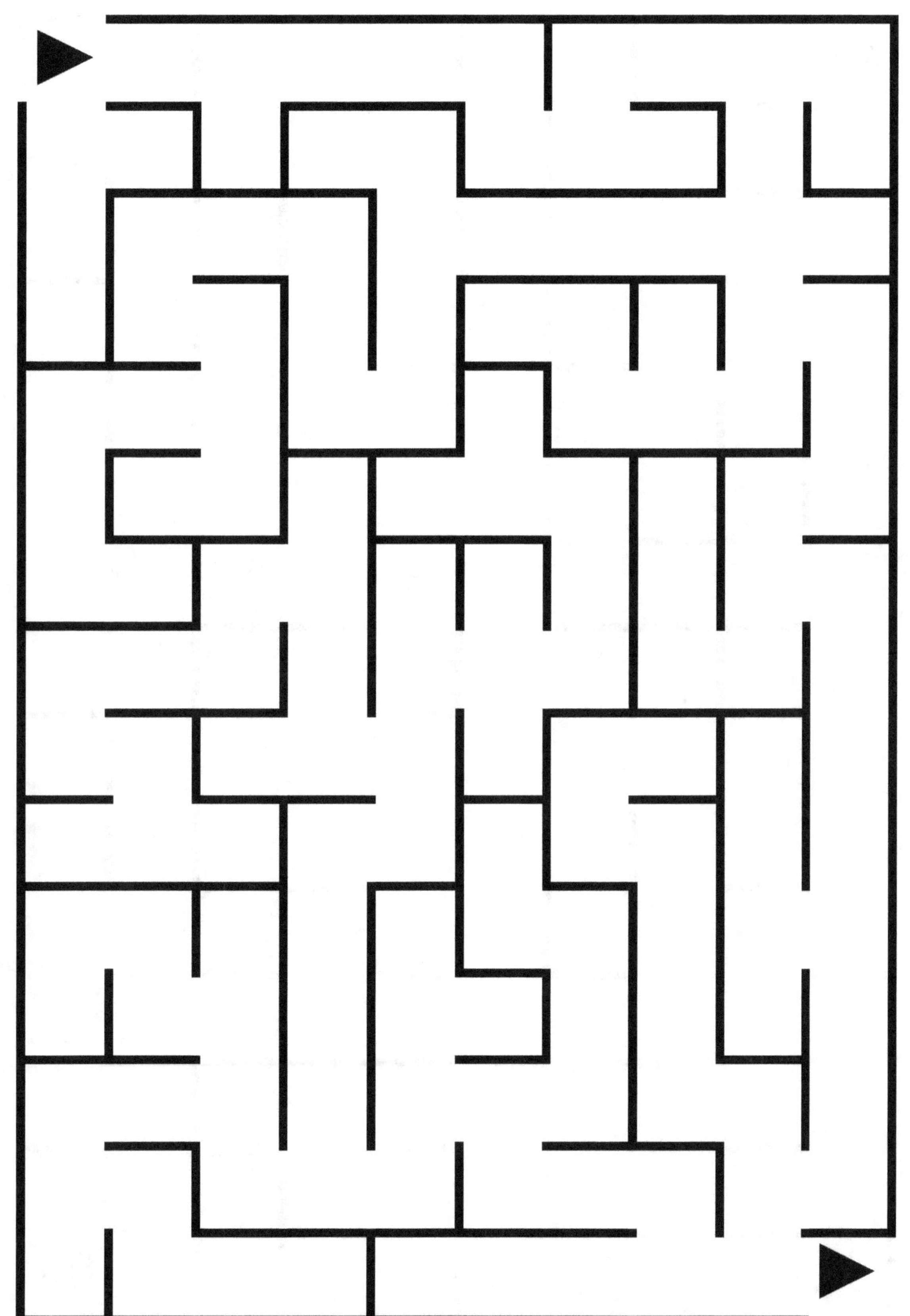

puzzle 49

puzzle 50

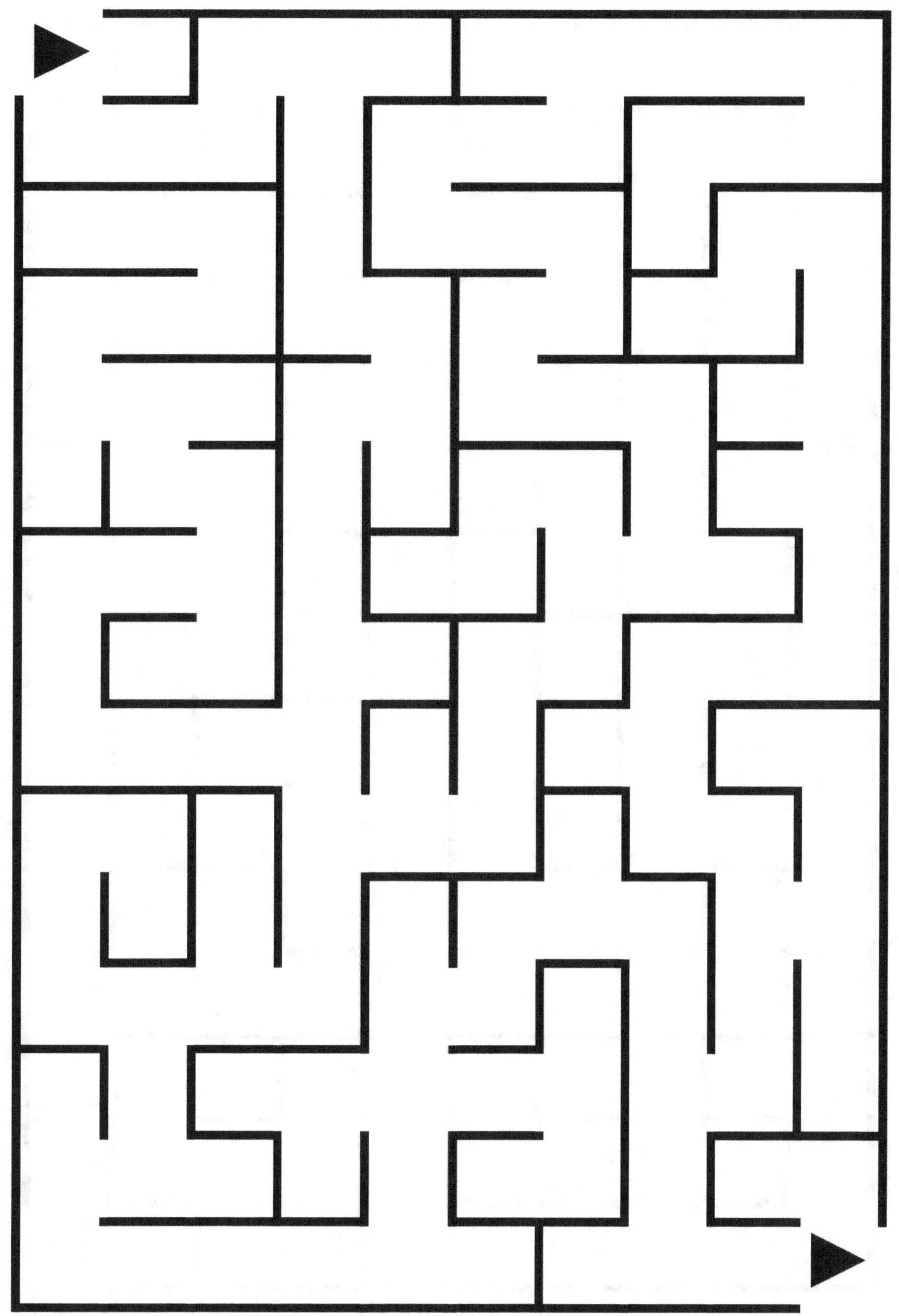

puzzle 51

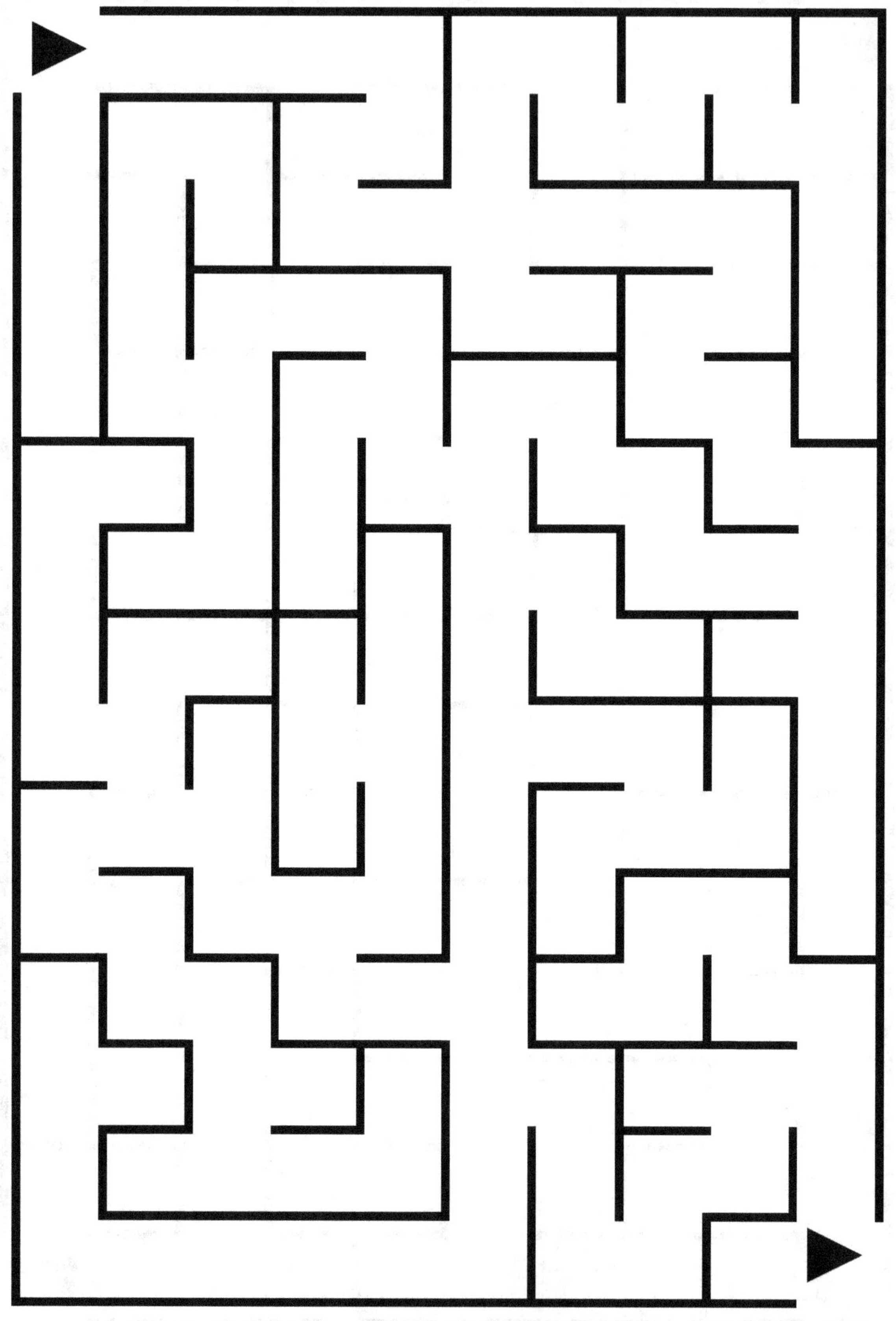

puzzle 52

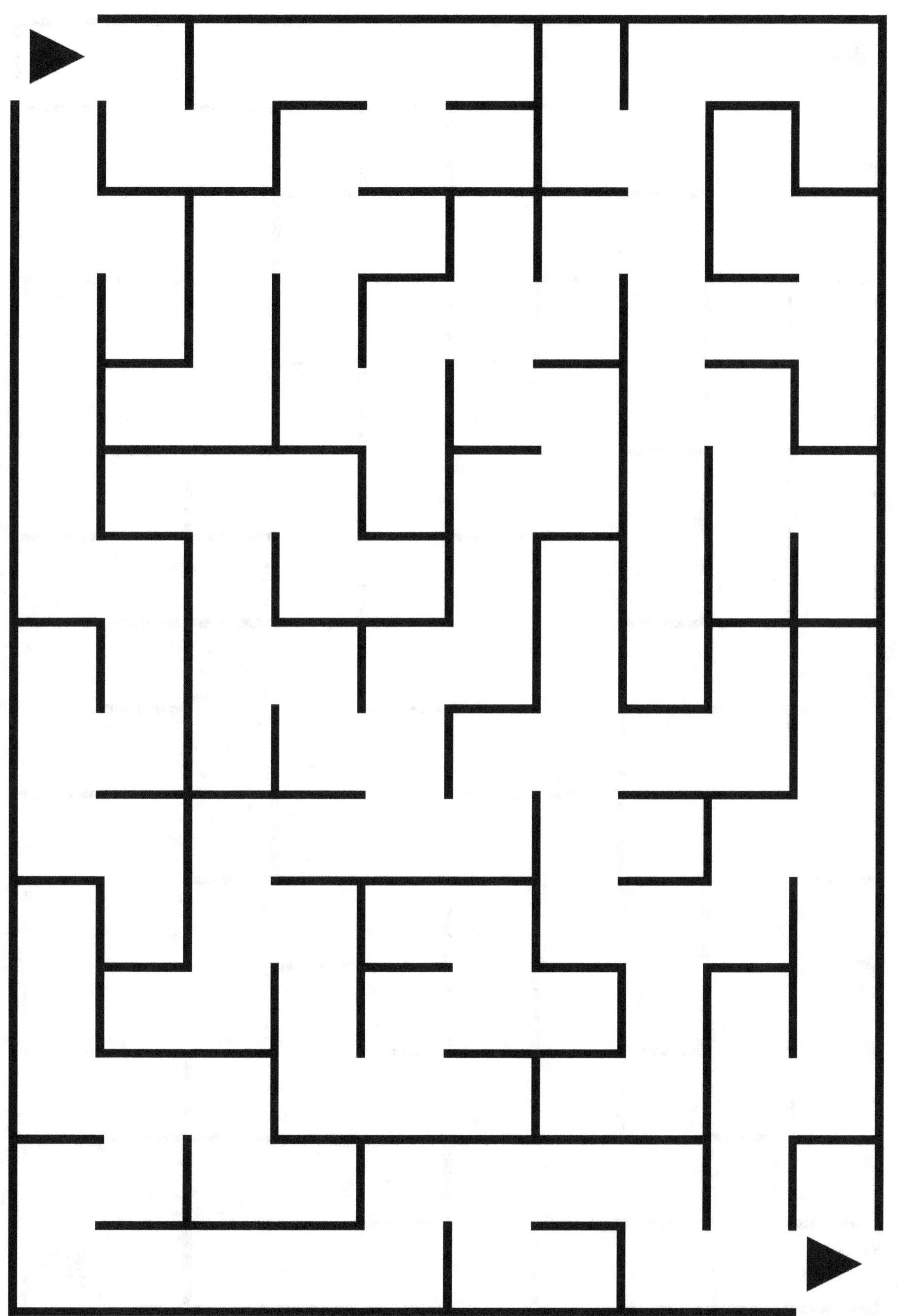

puzzle 53

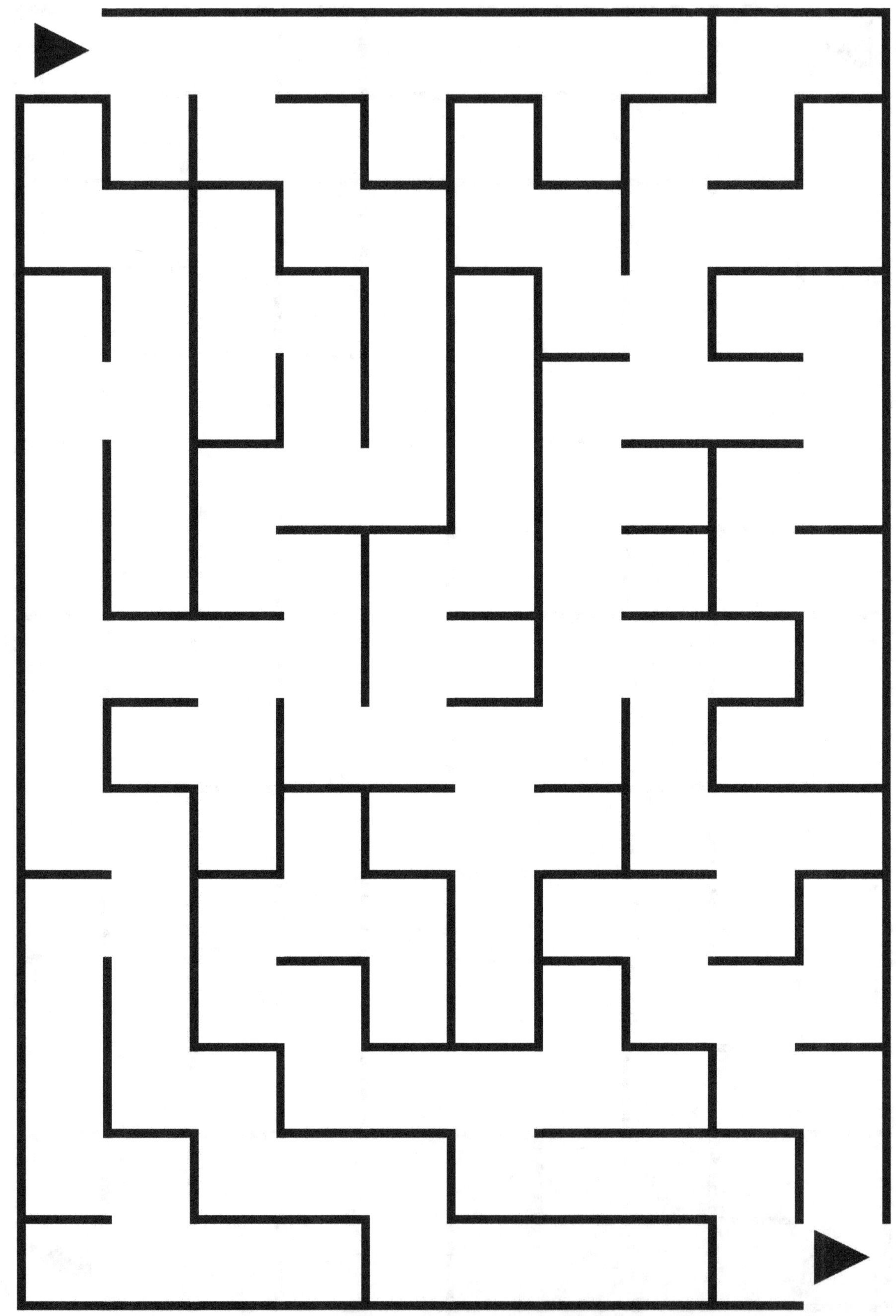

puzzle 54

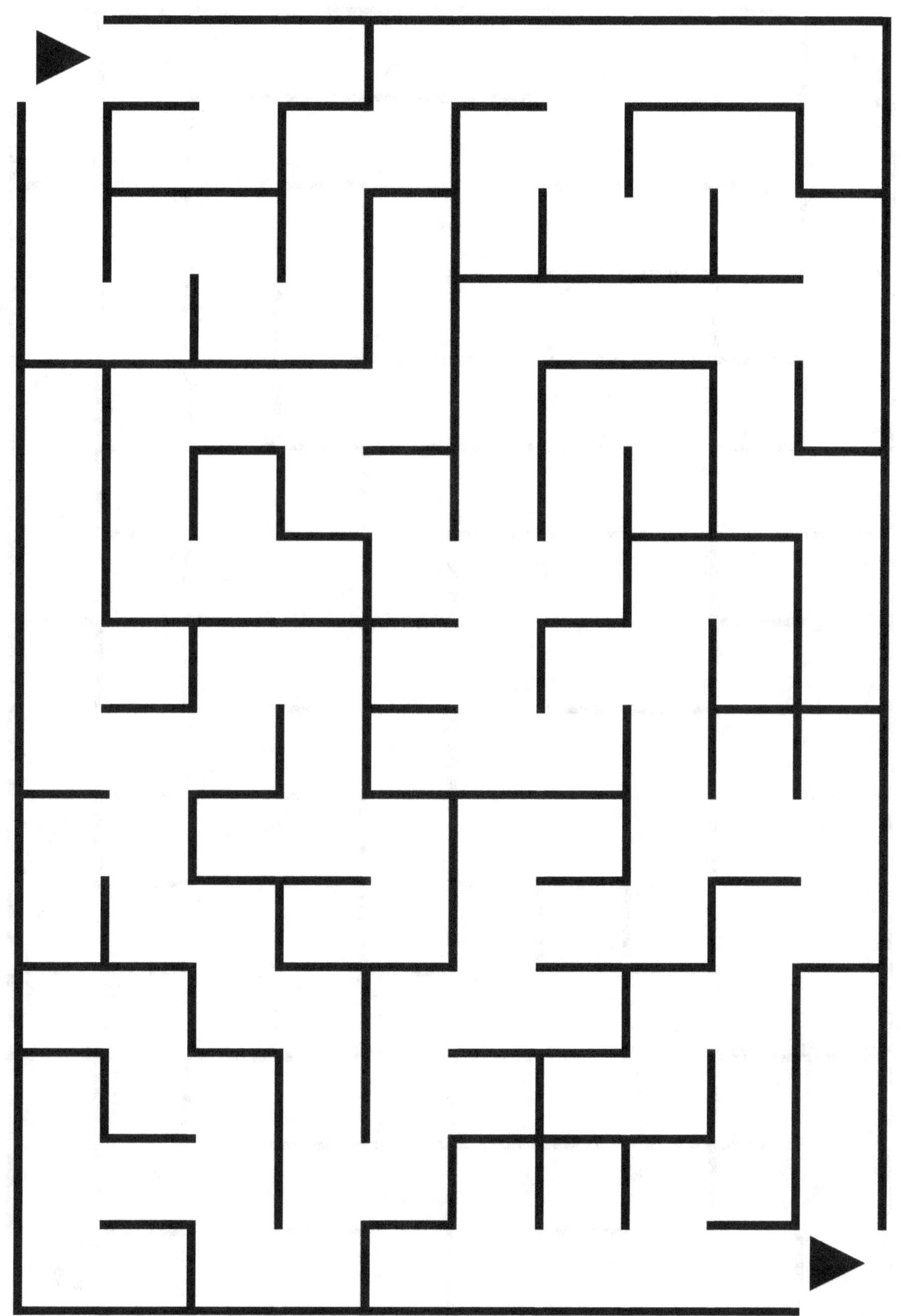

puzzle 55

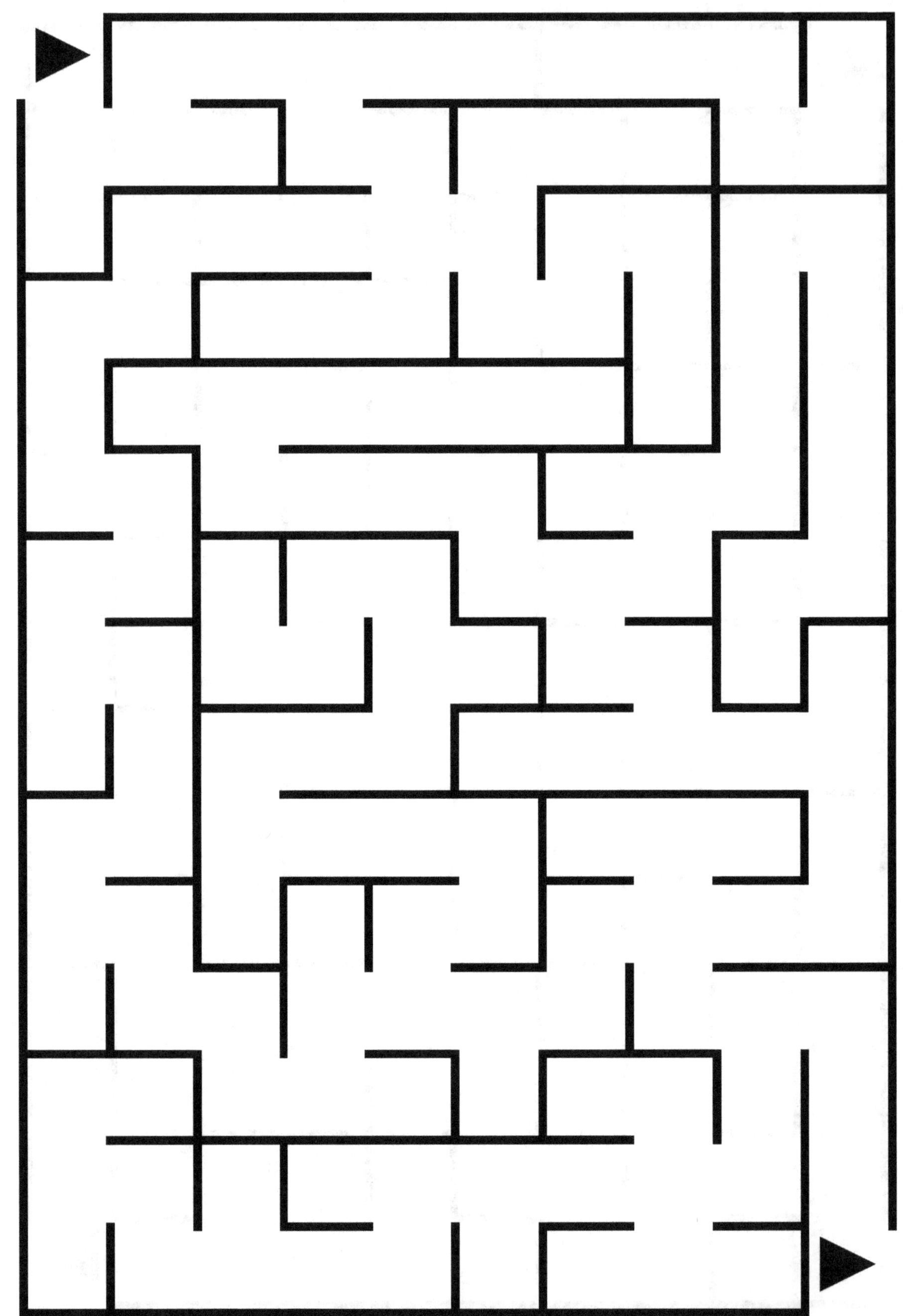

puzzle 56

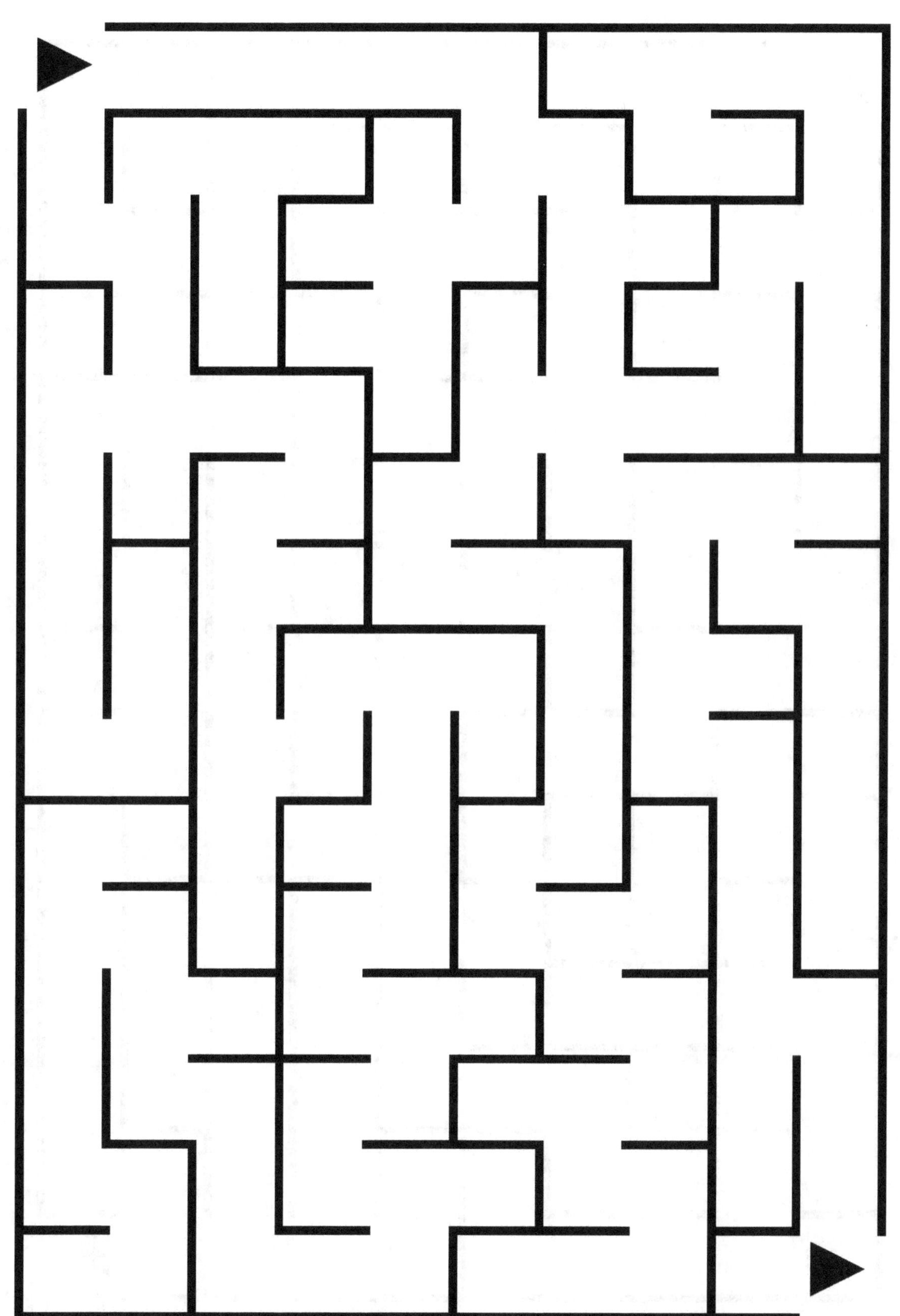

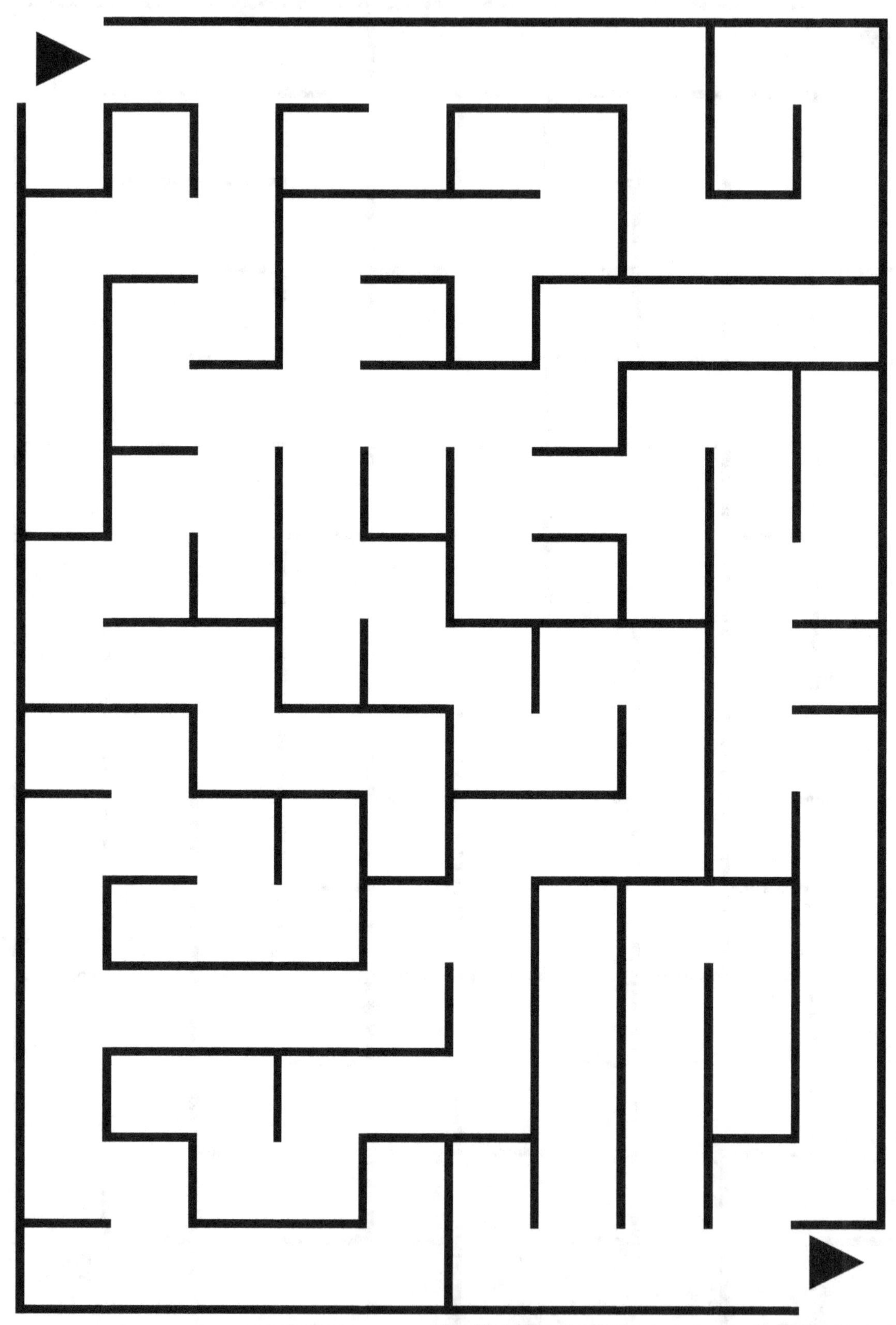

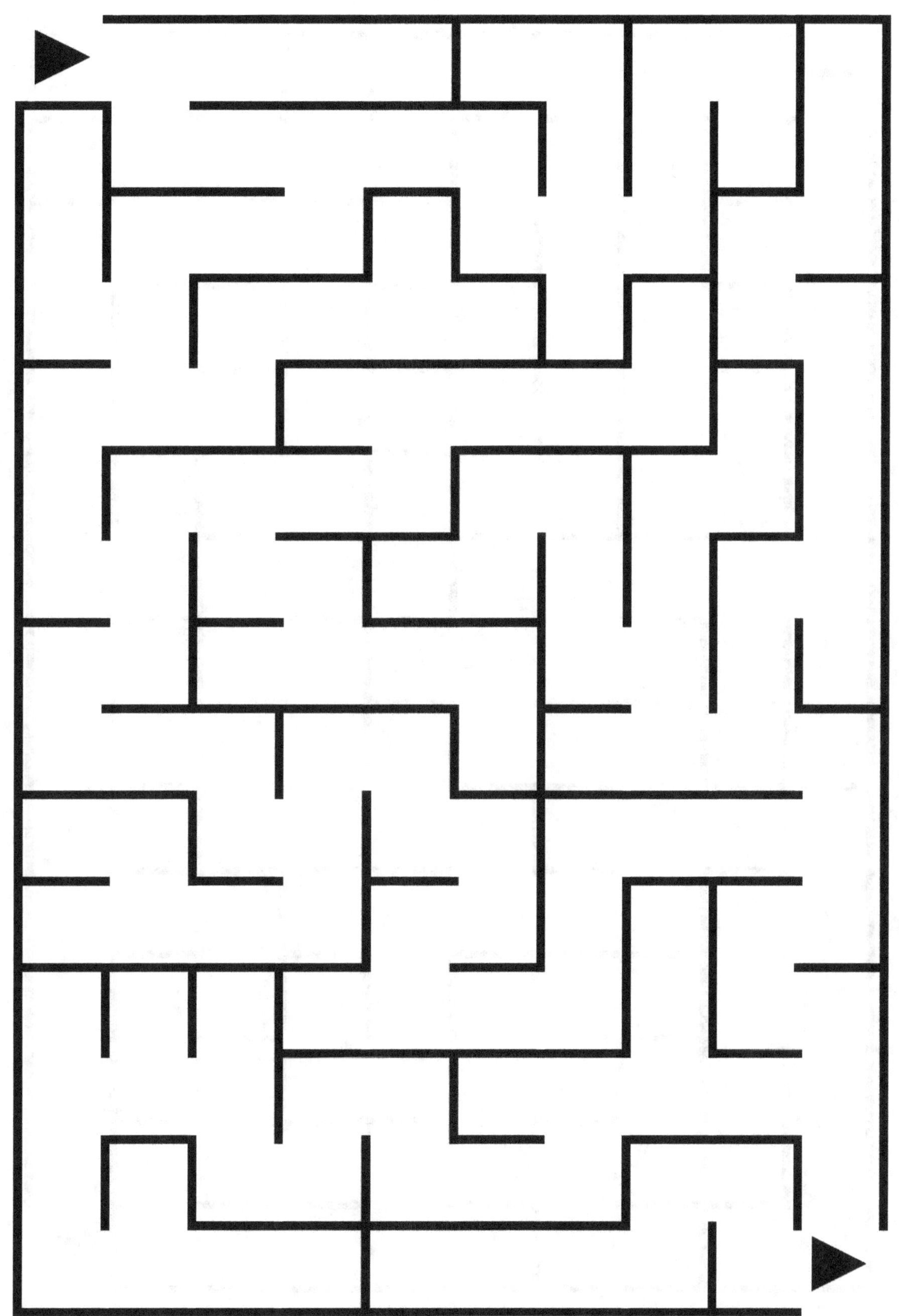

puzzle 59

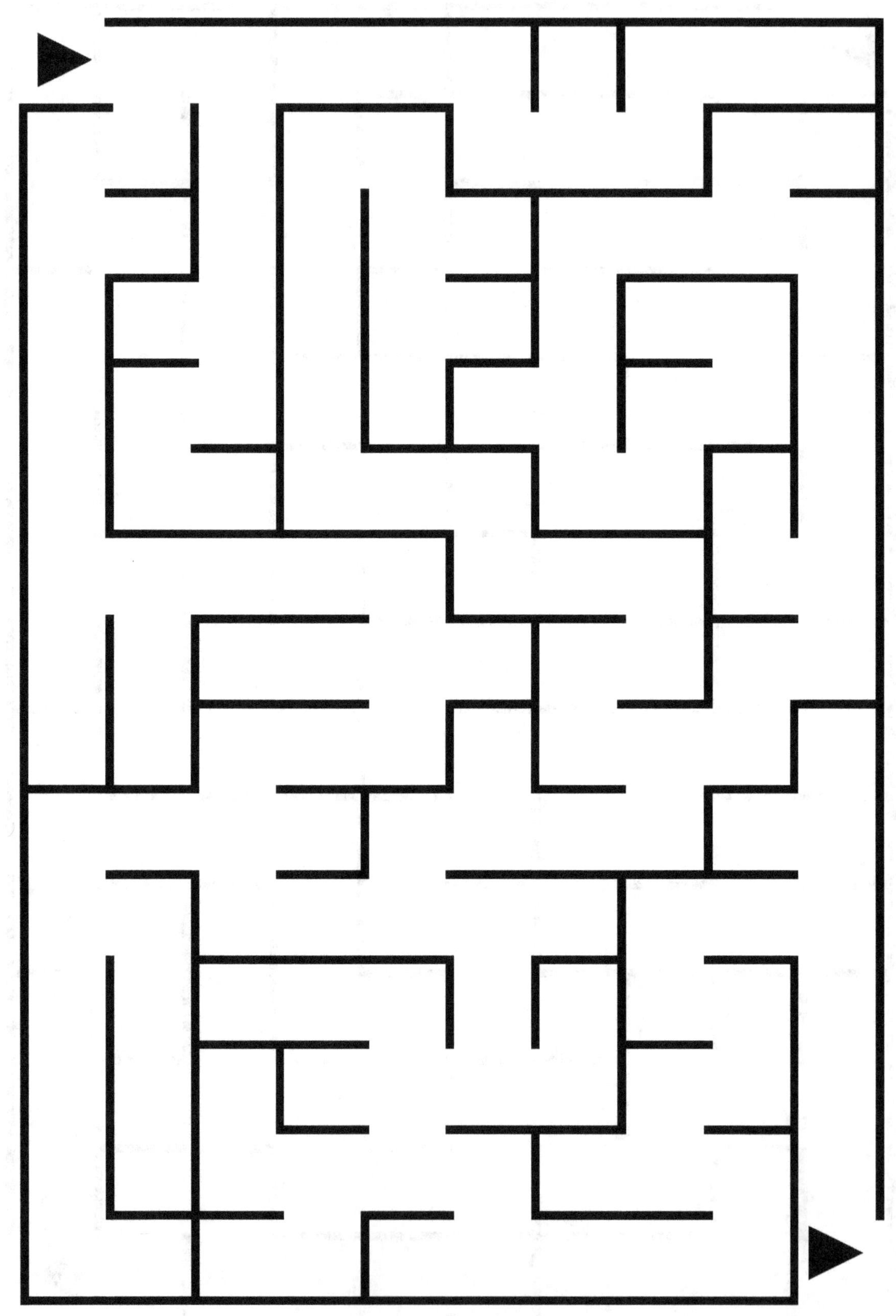

puzzle 60

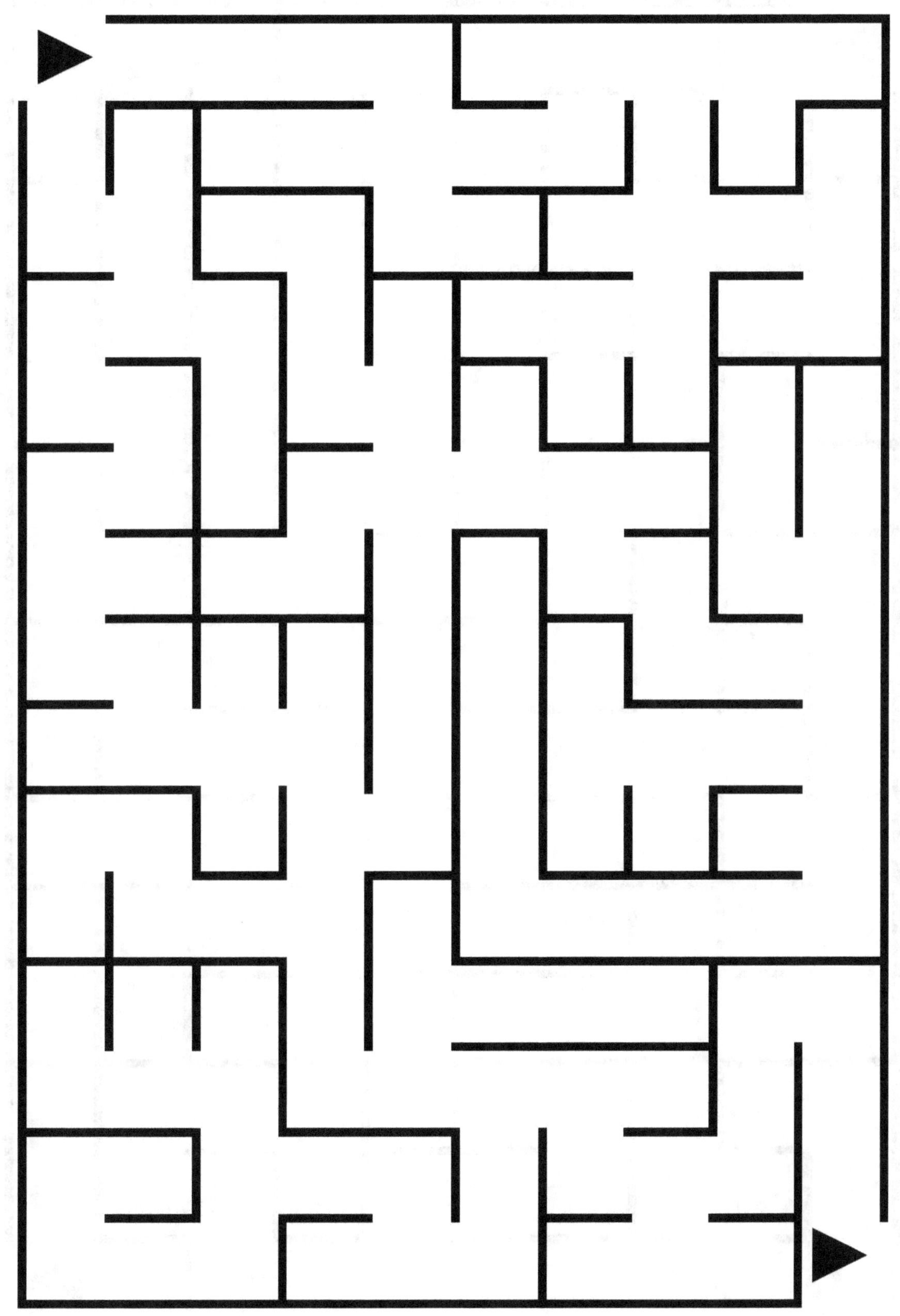

puzzle 61

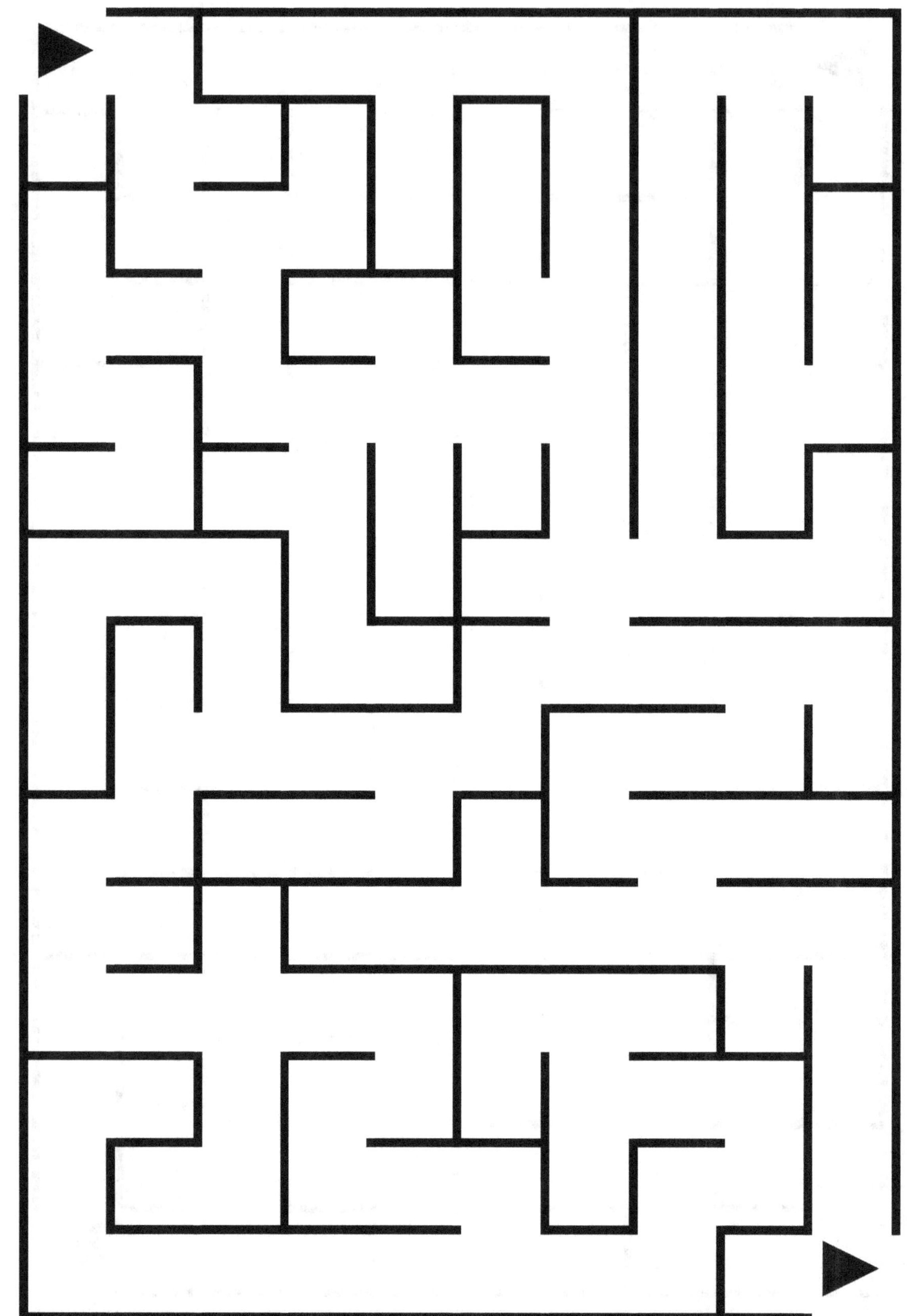

puzzle 62

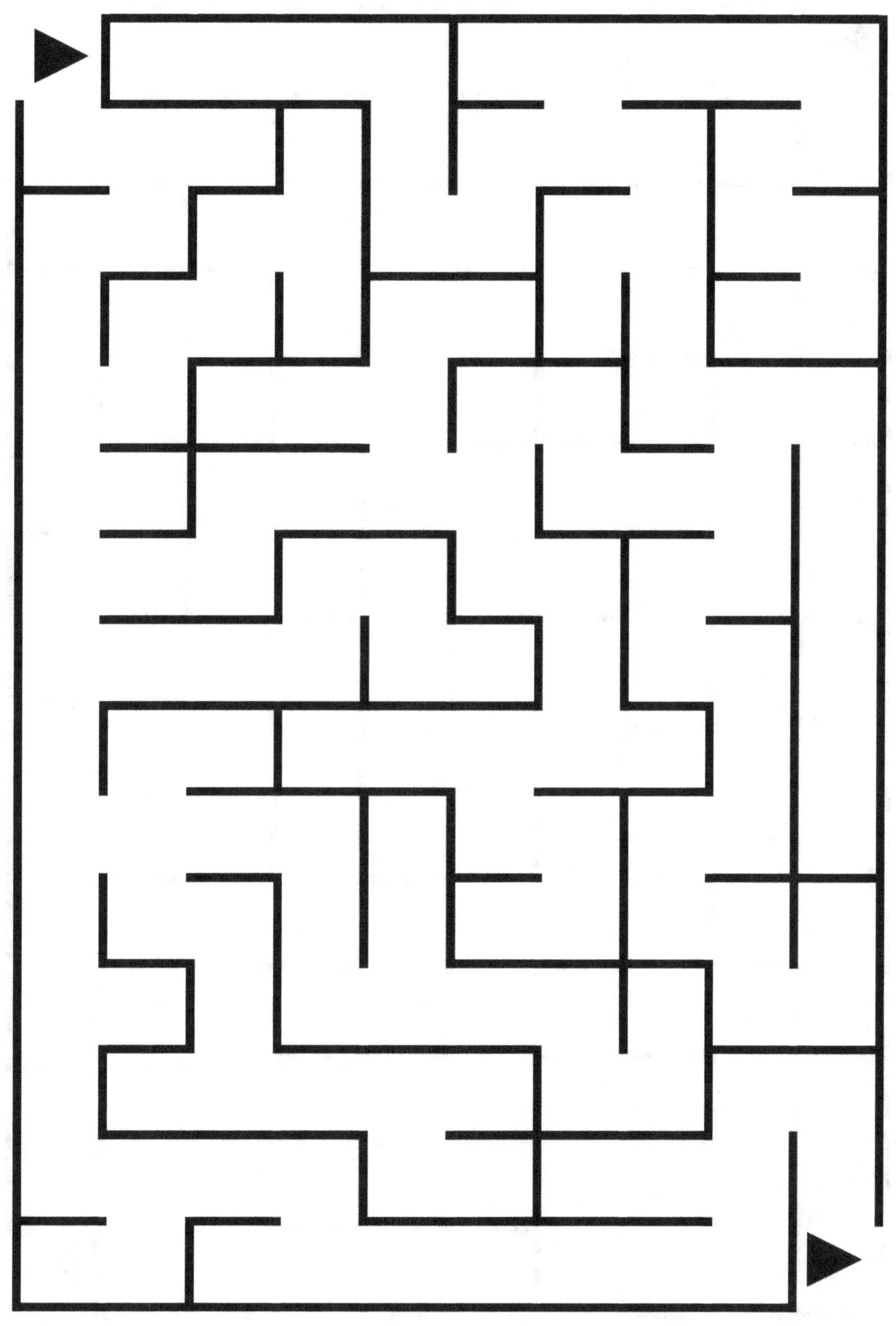

puzzle 63

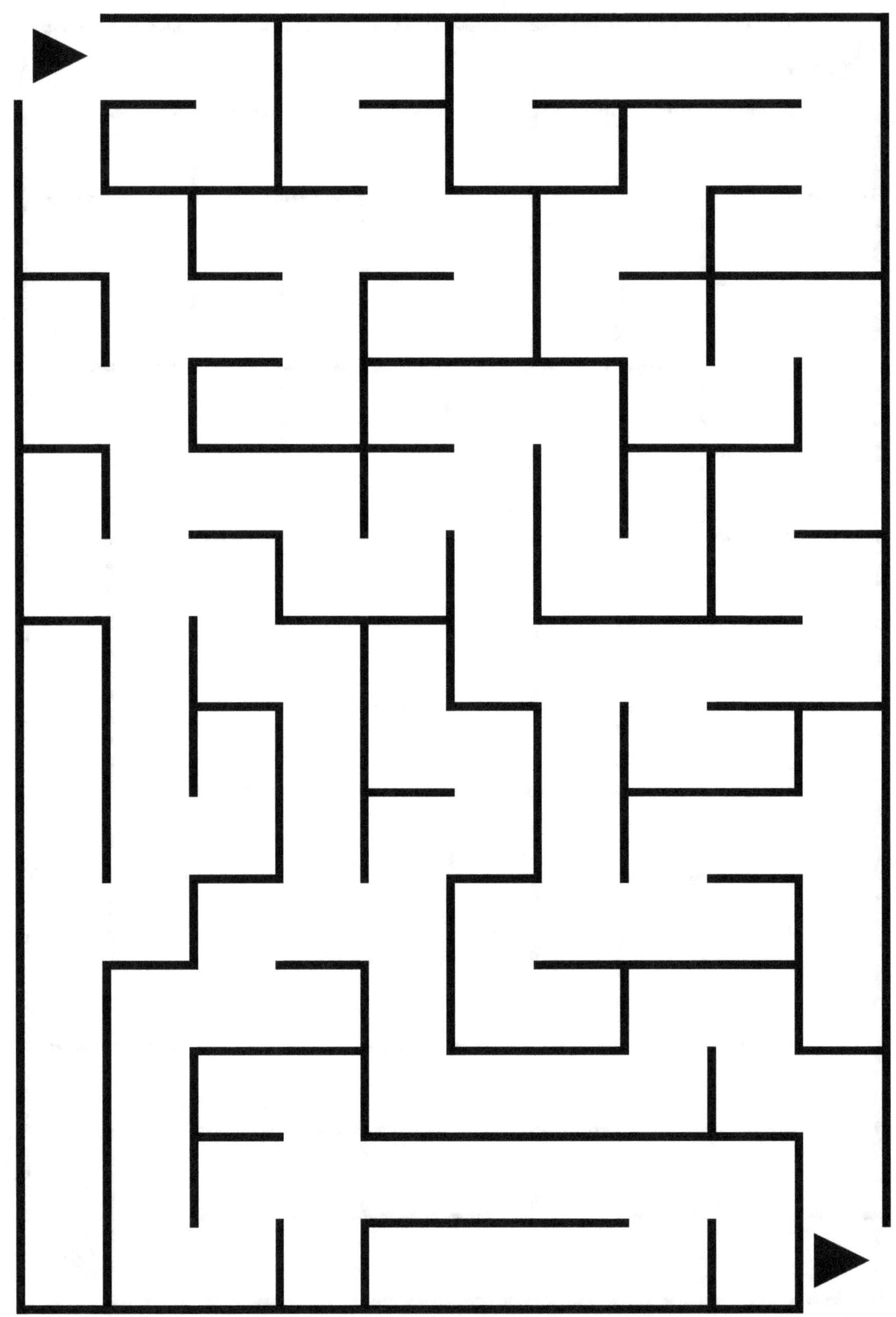

puzzle 64

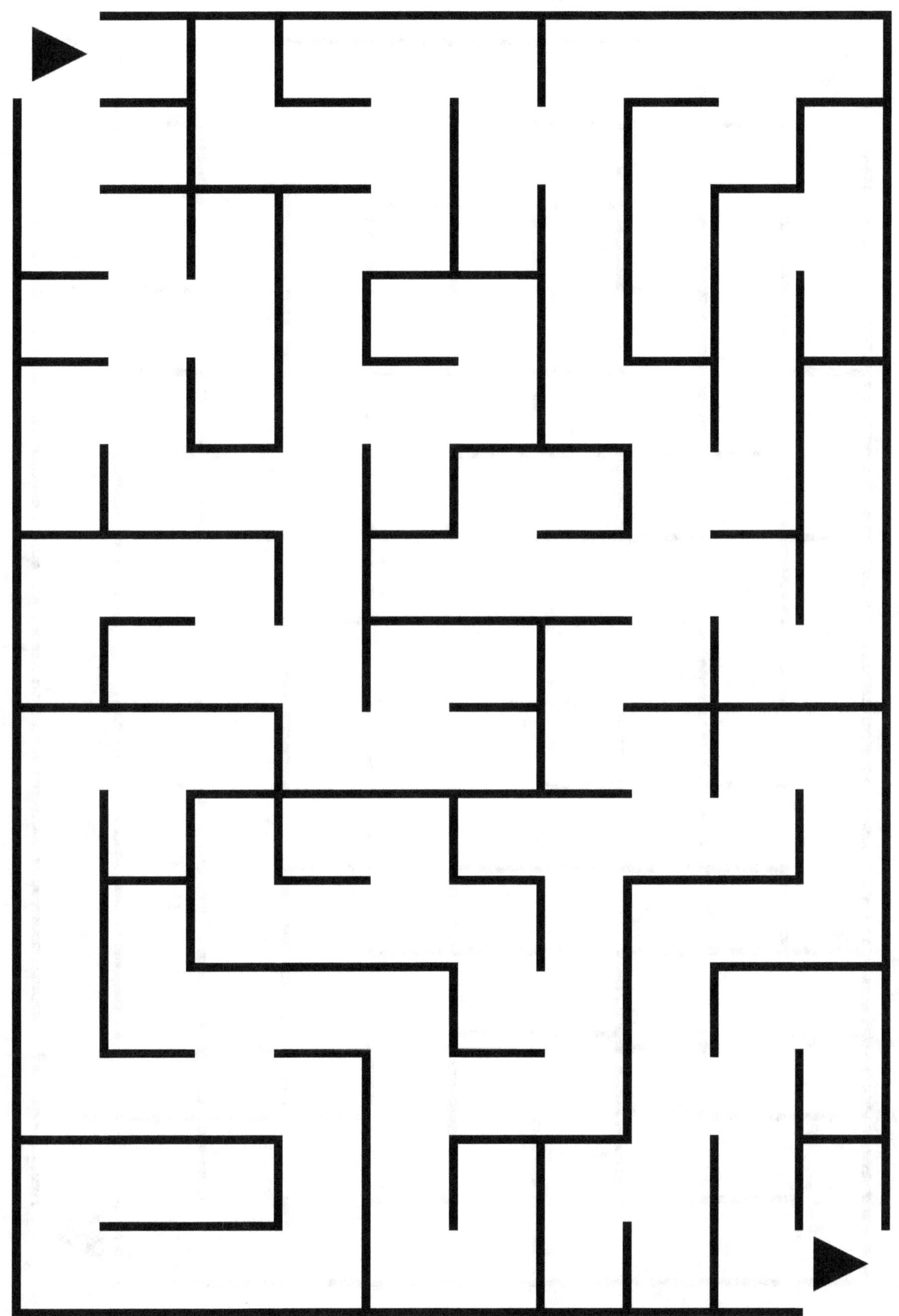

puzzle 65

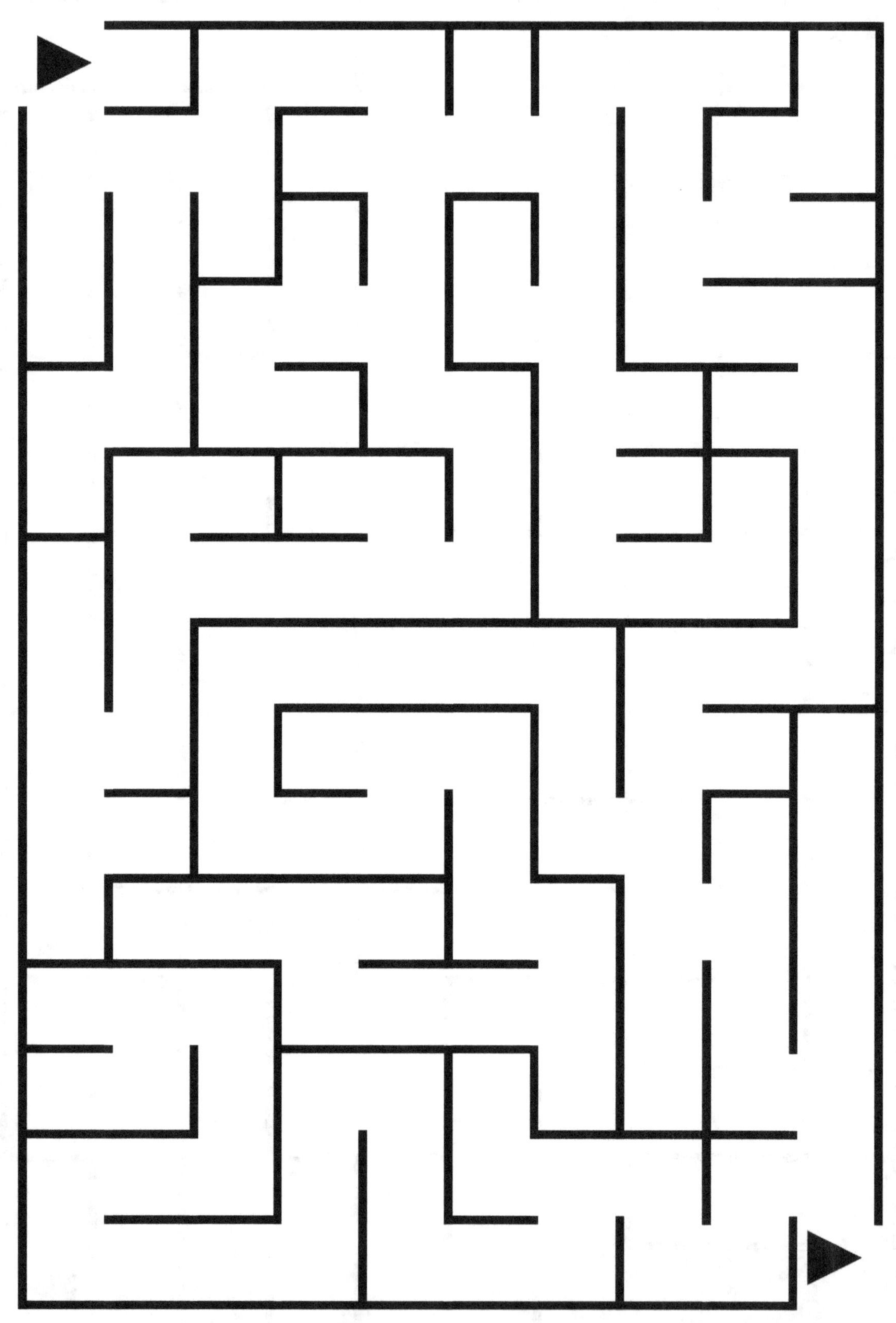

puzzle 66

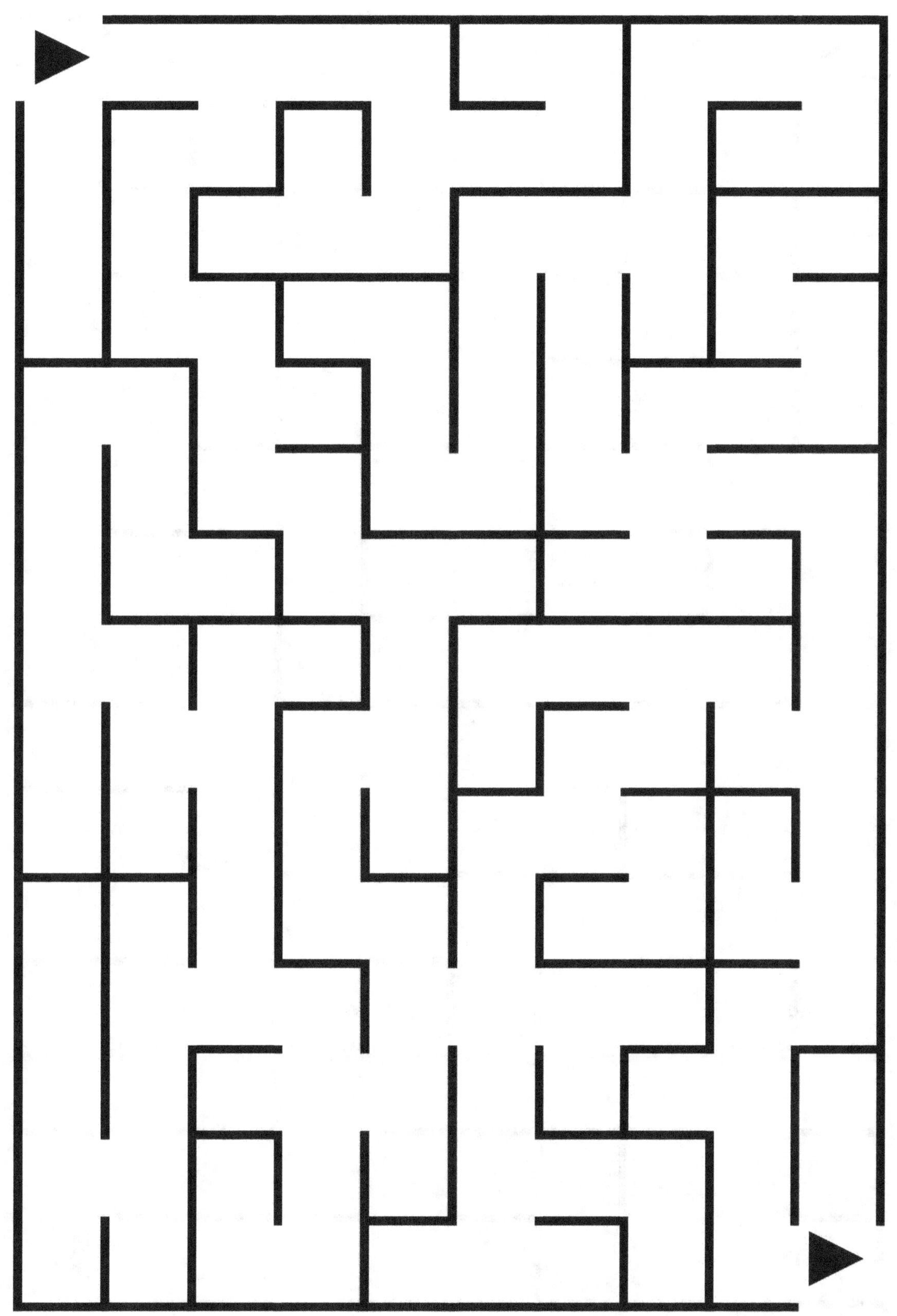

puzzle 67

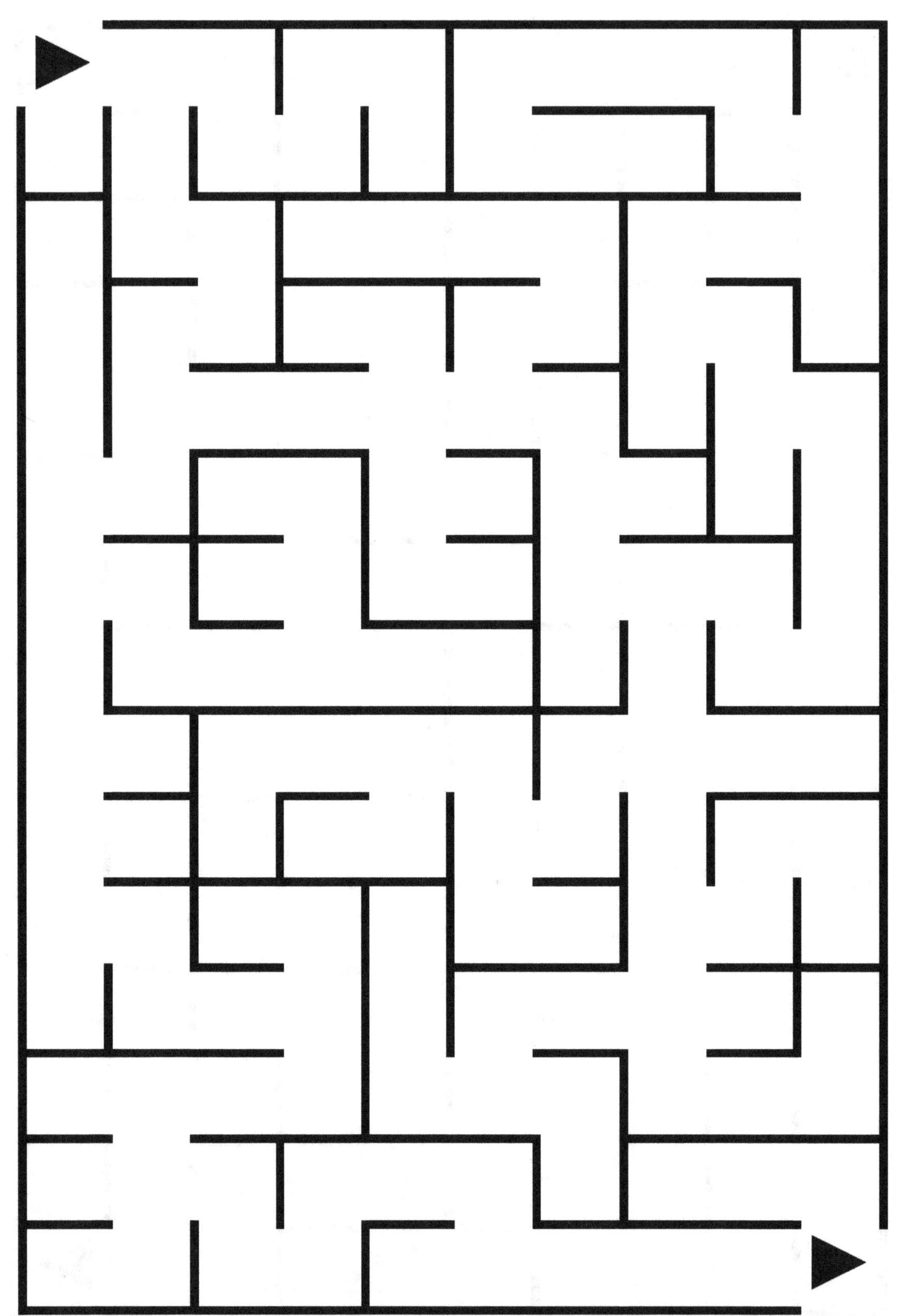

puzzle 68

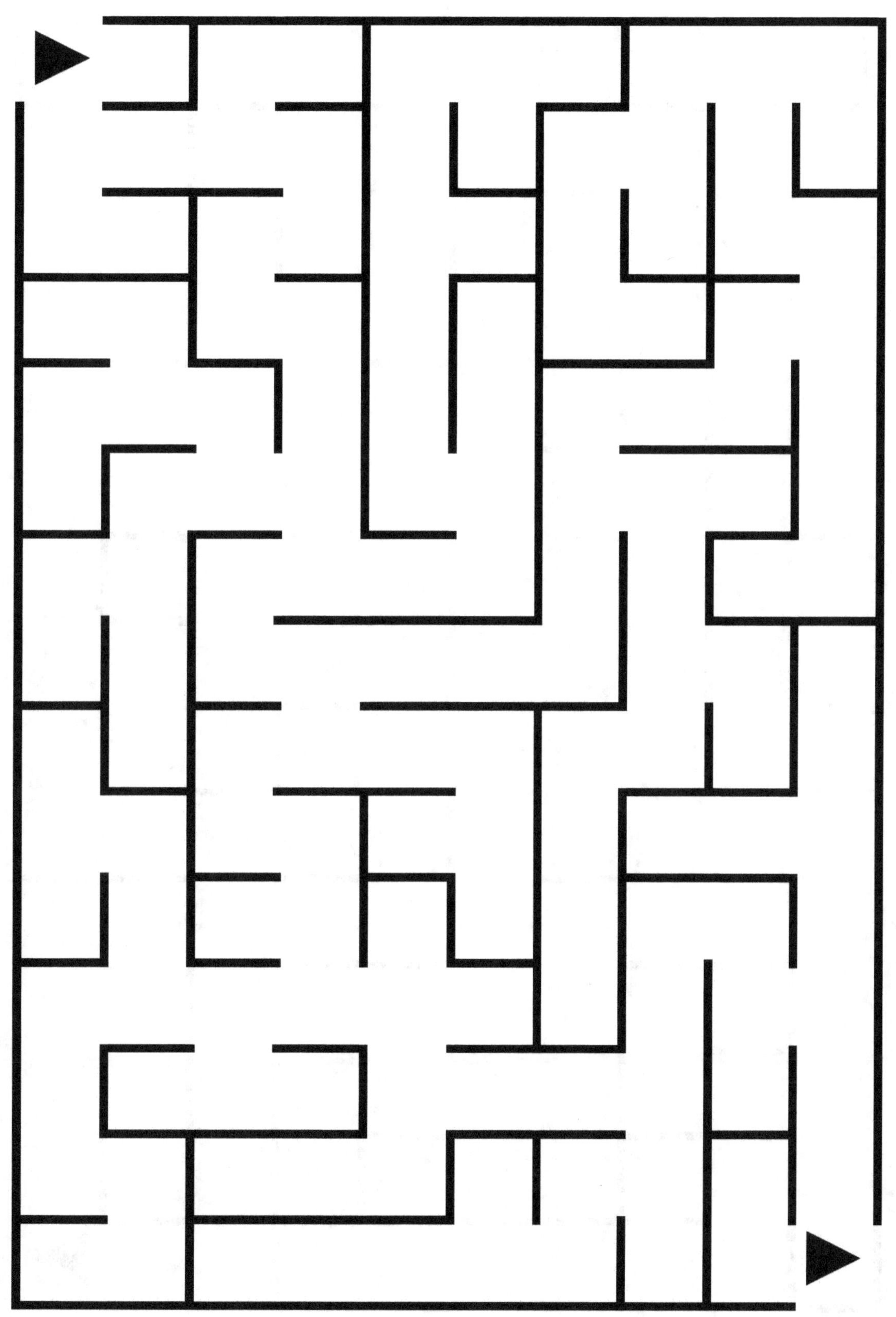

puzzle 69

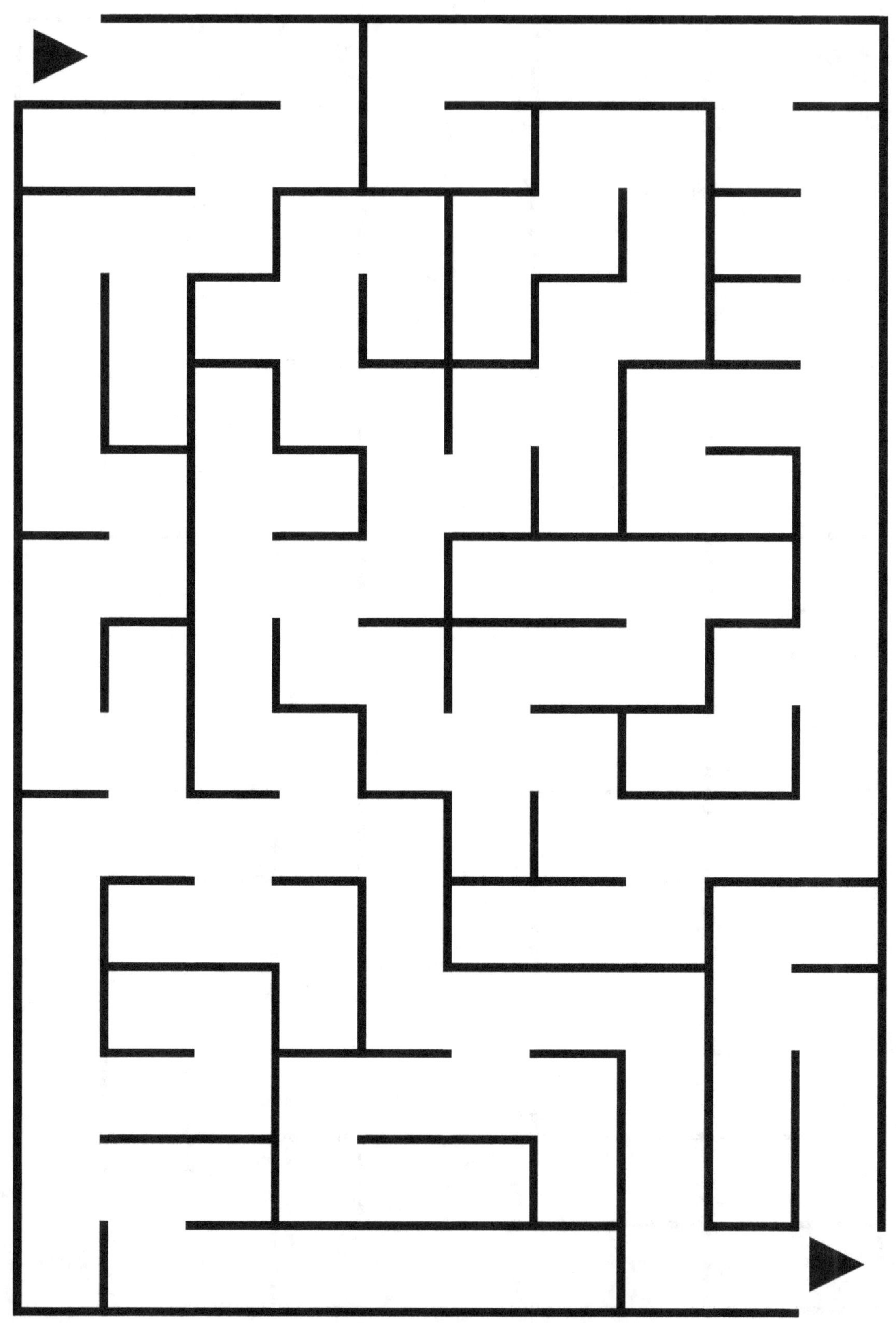

puzzle 70

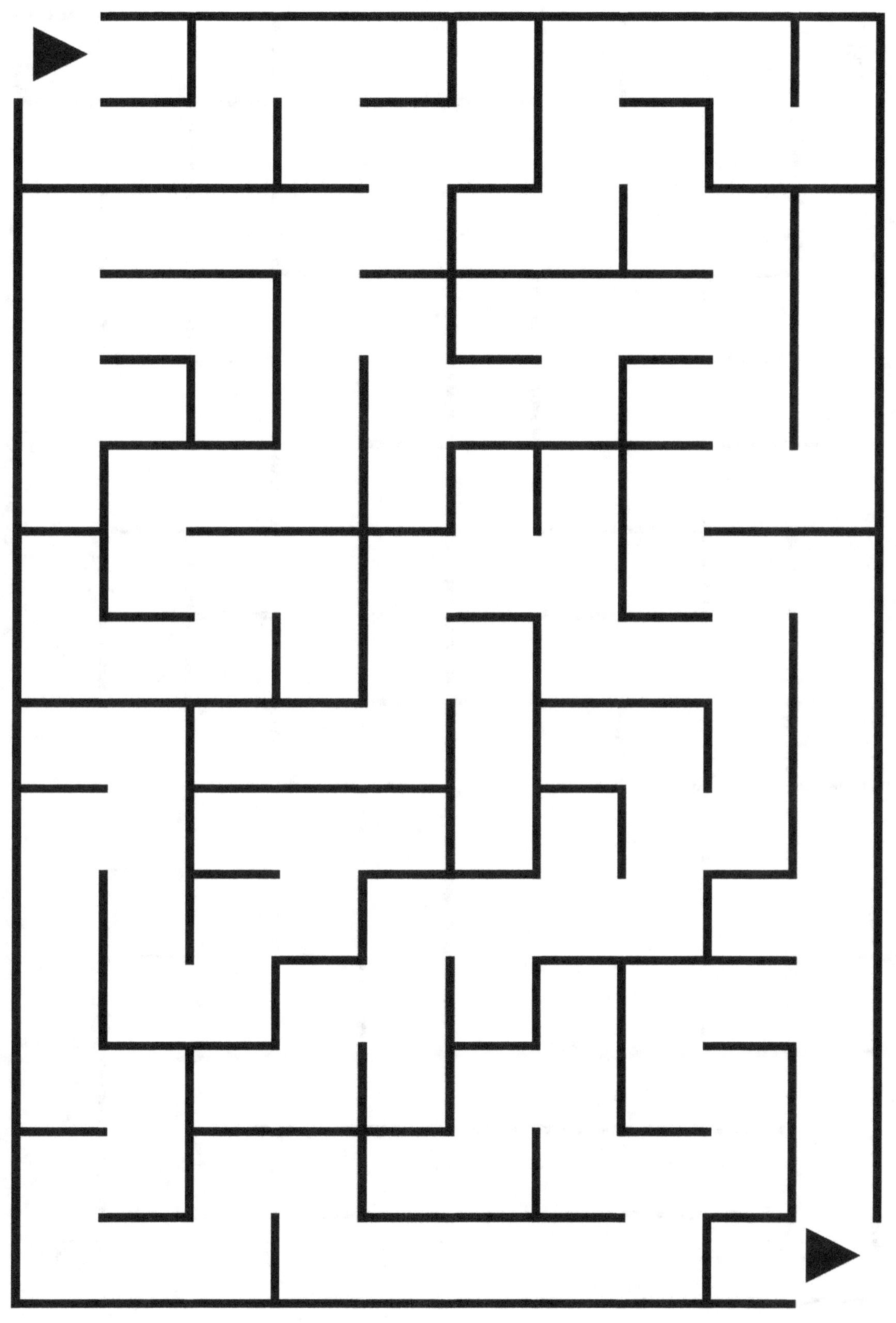

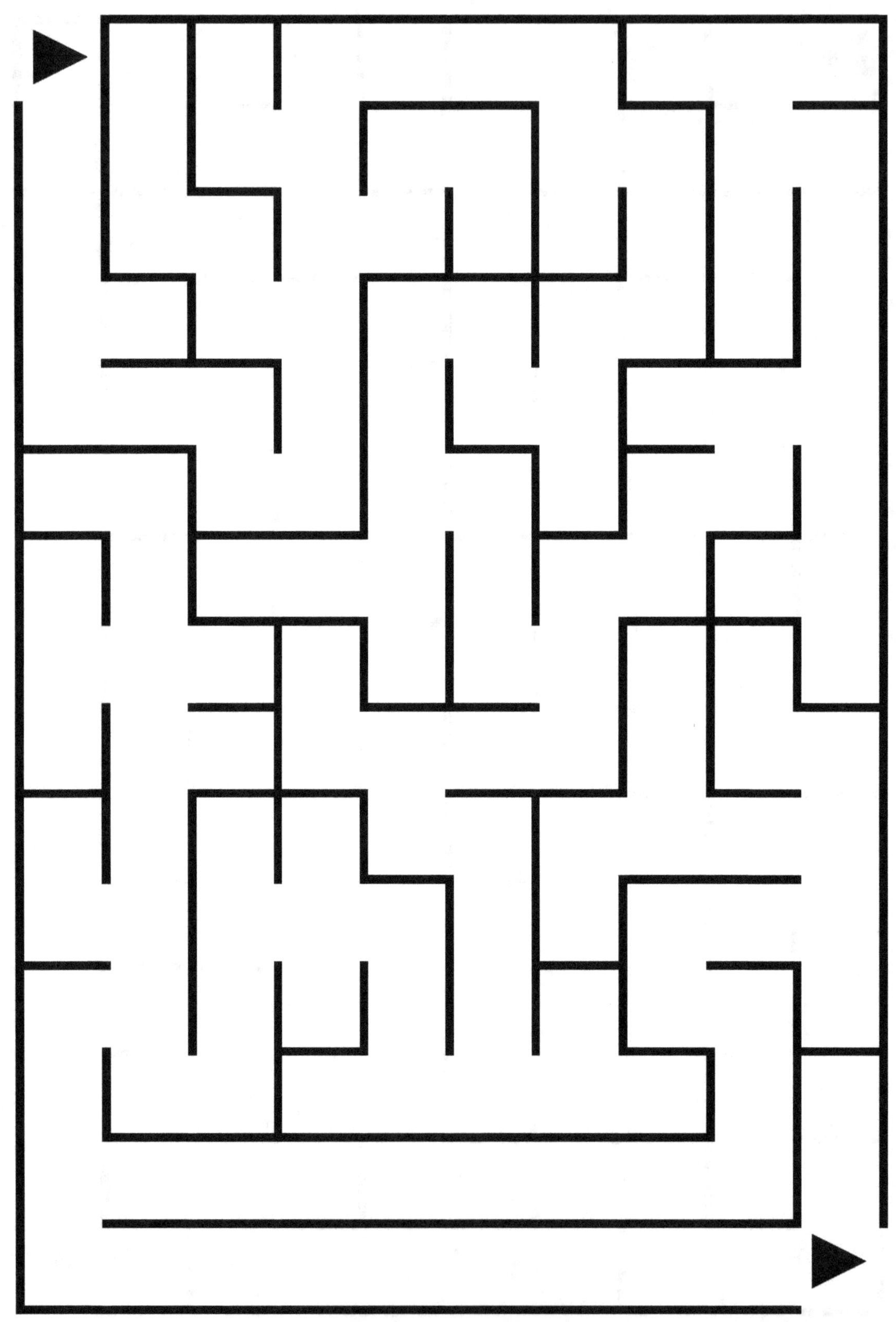

puzzle 72

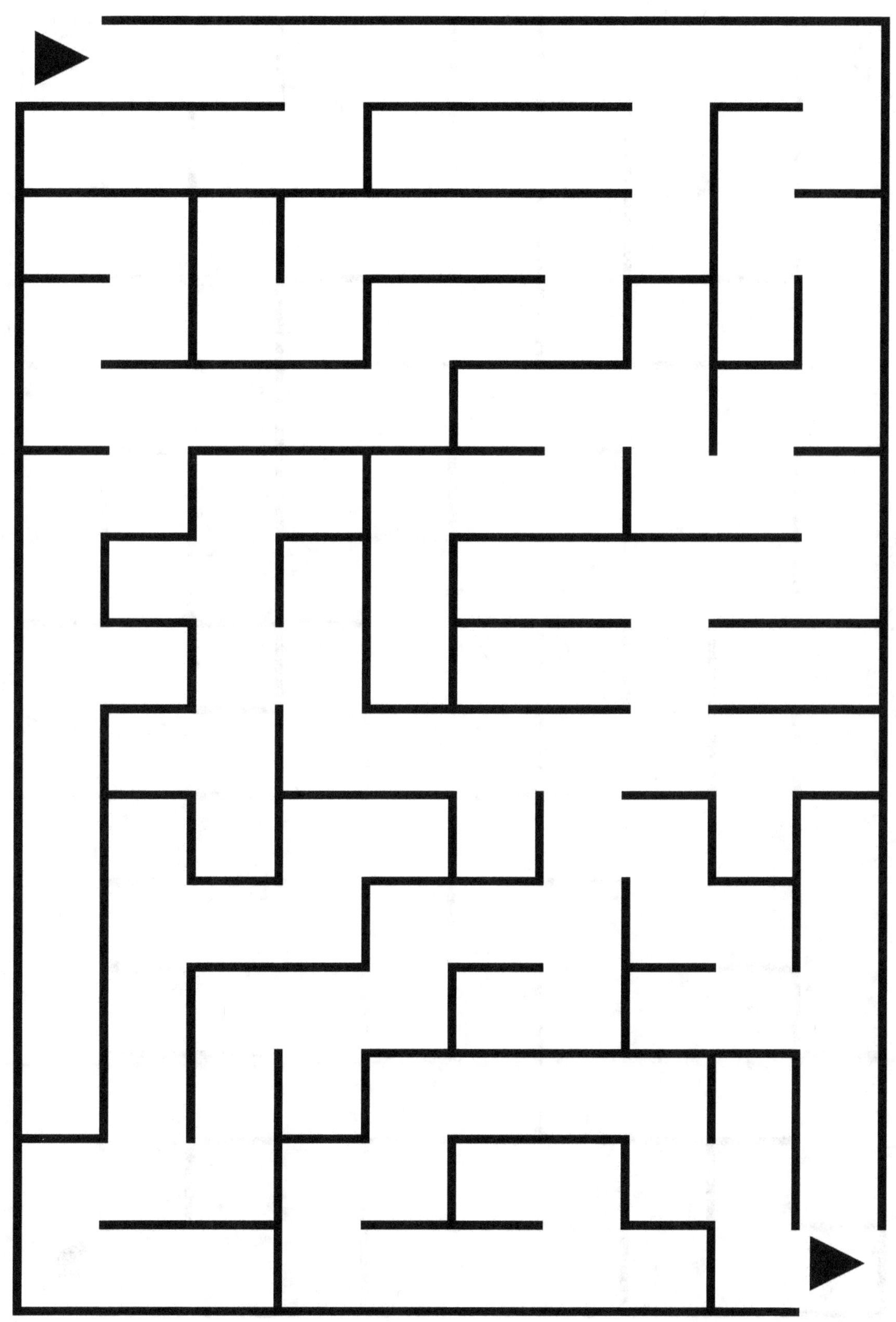

puzzle 73

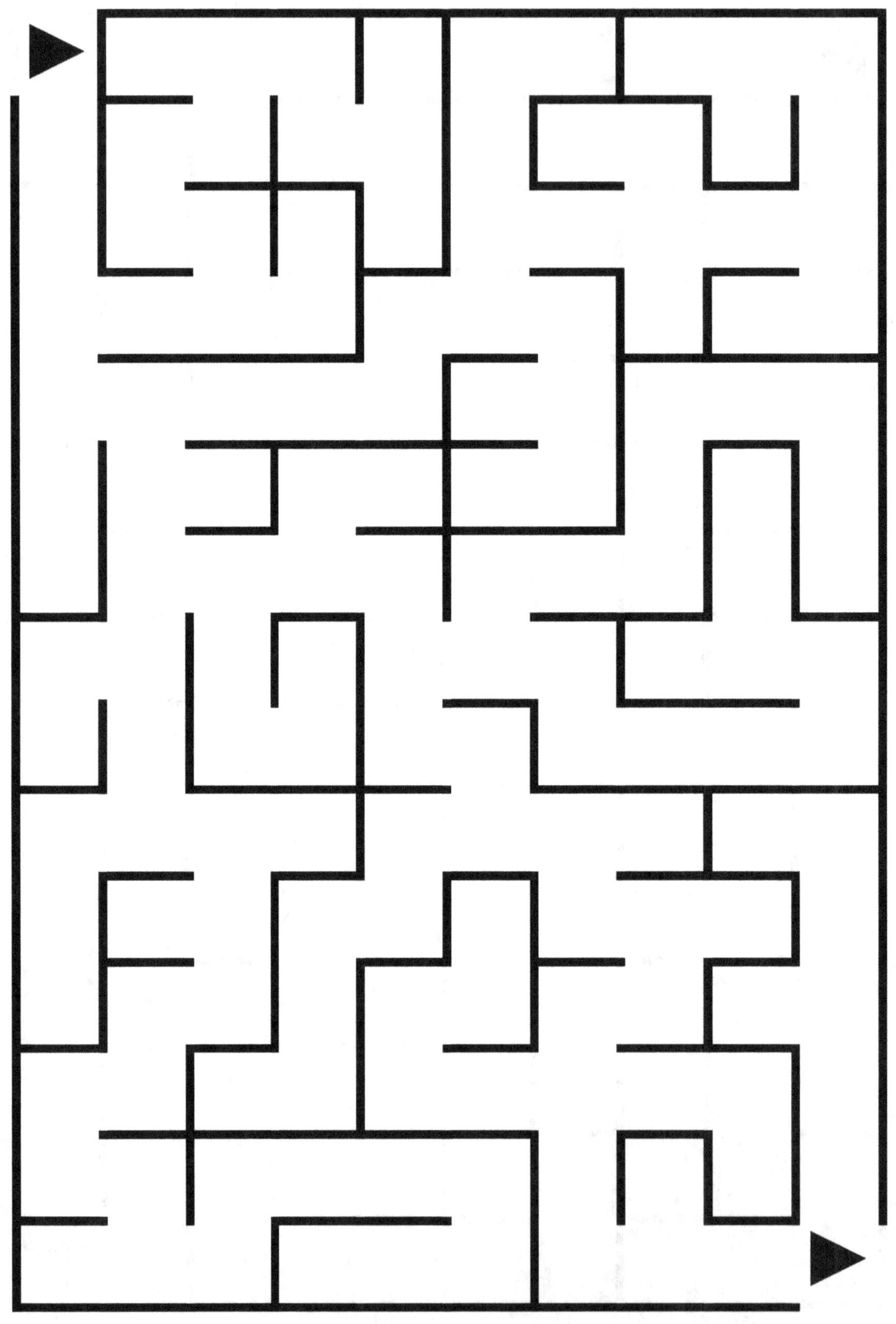

puzzle 74

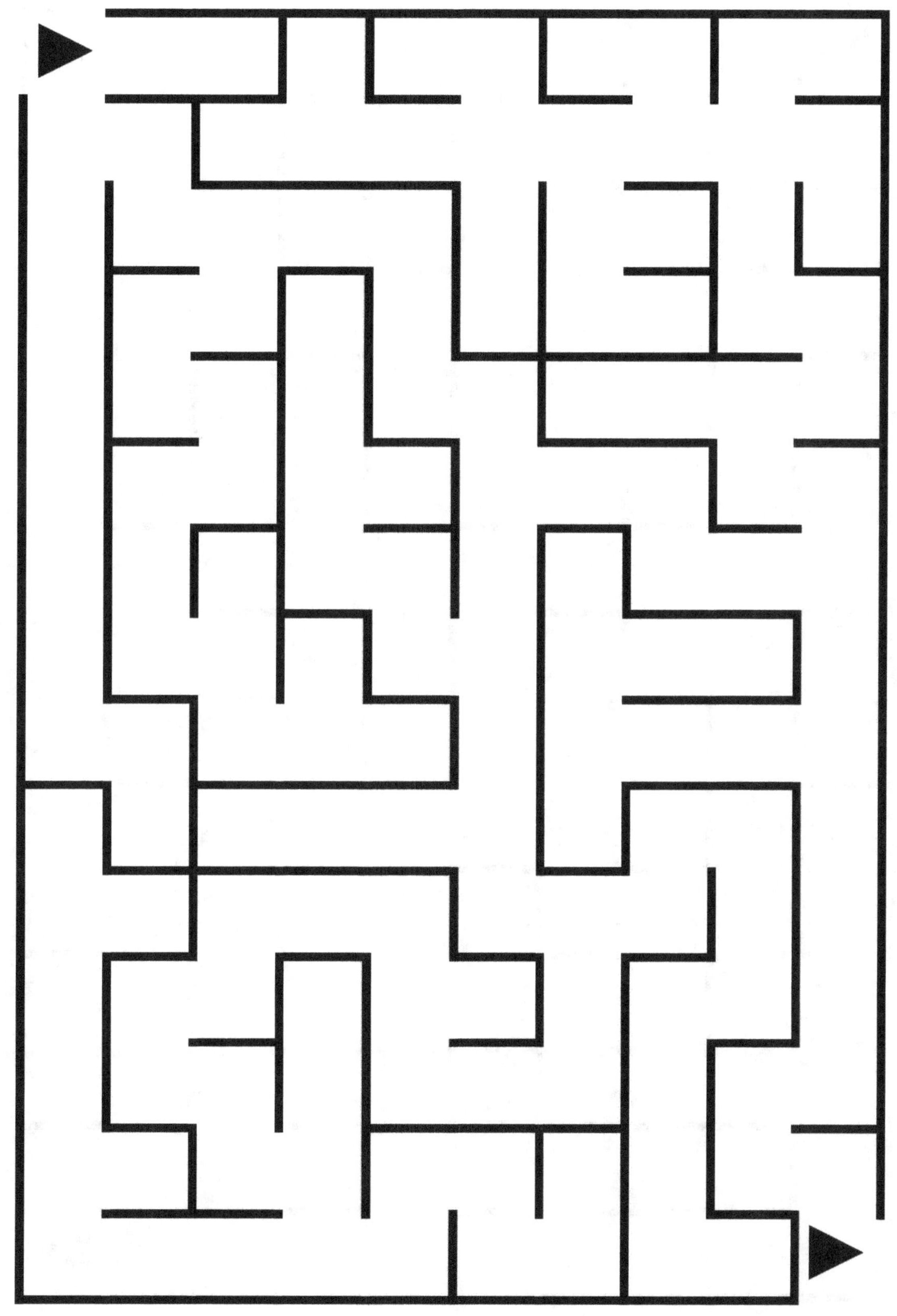

puzzle 75

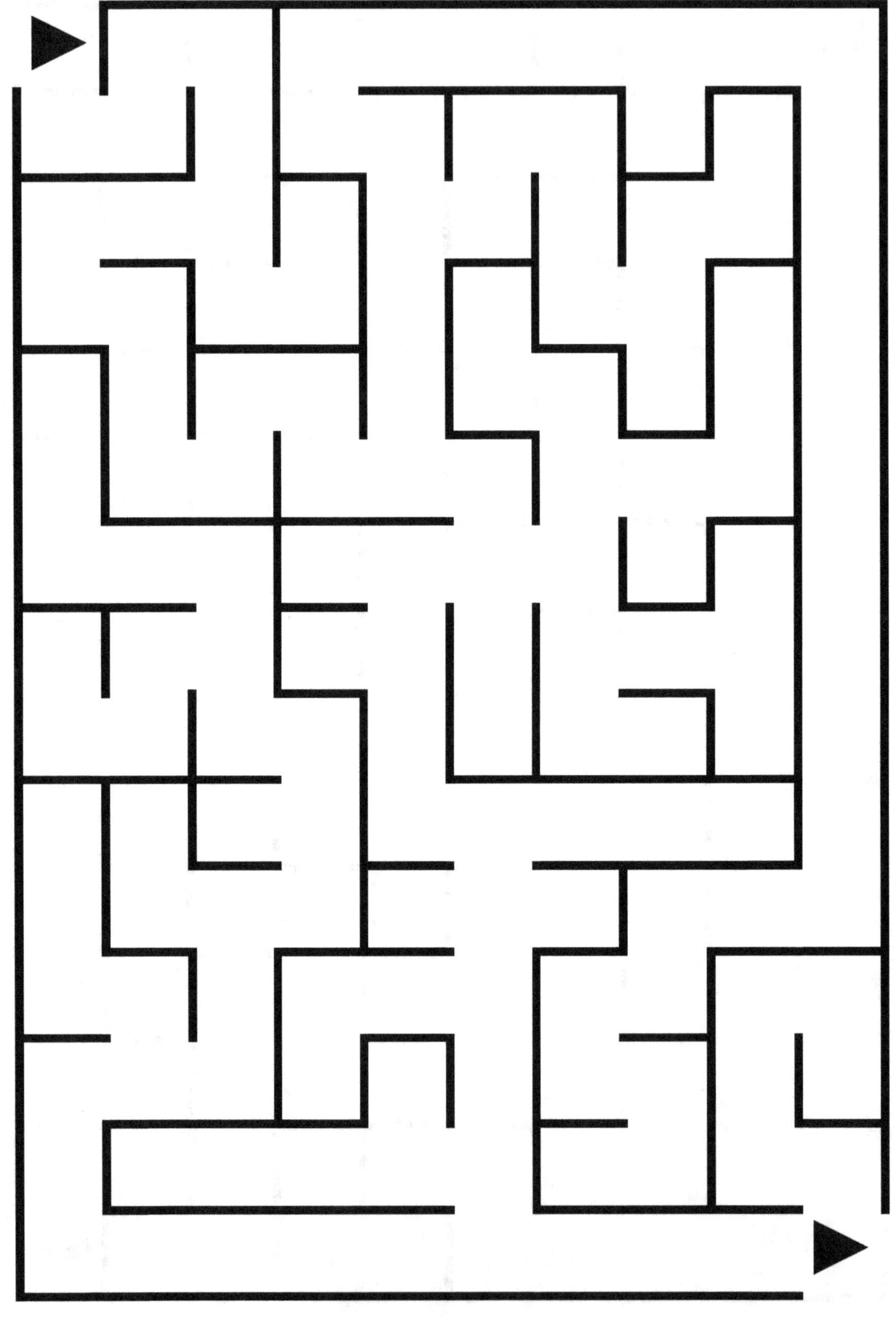

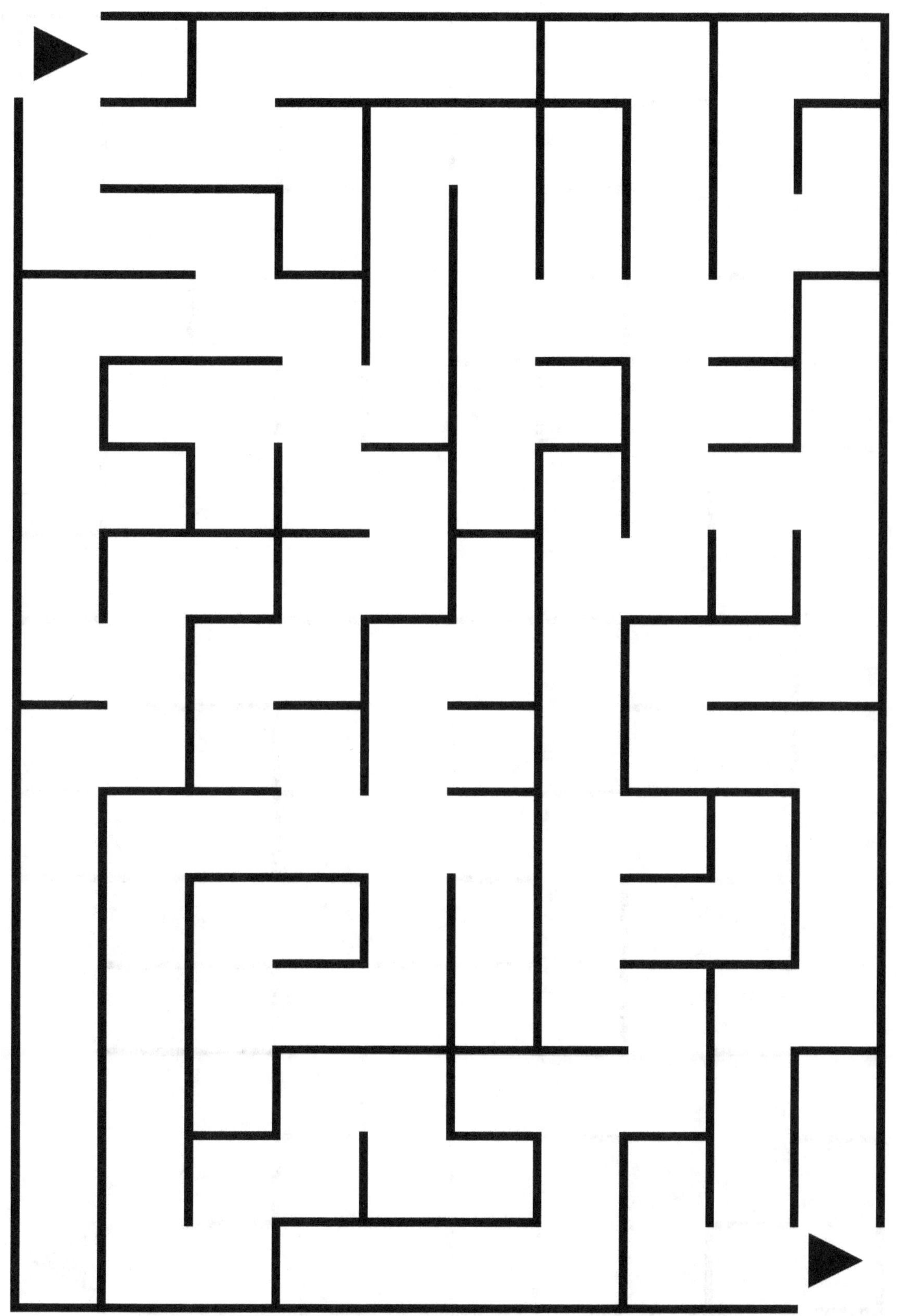

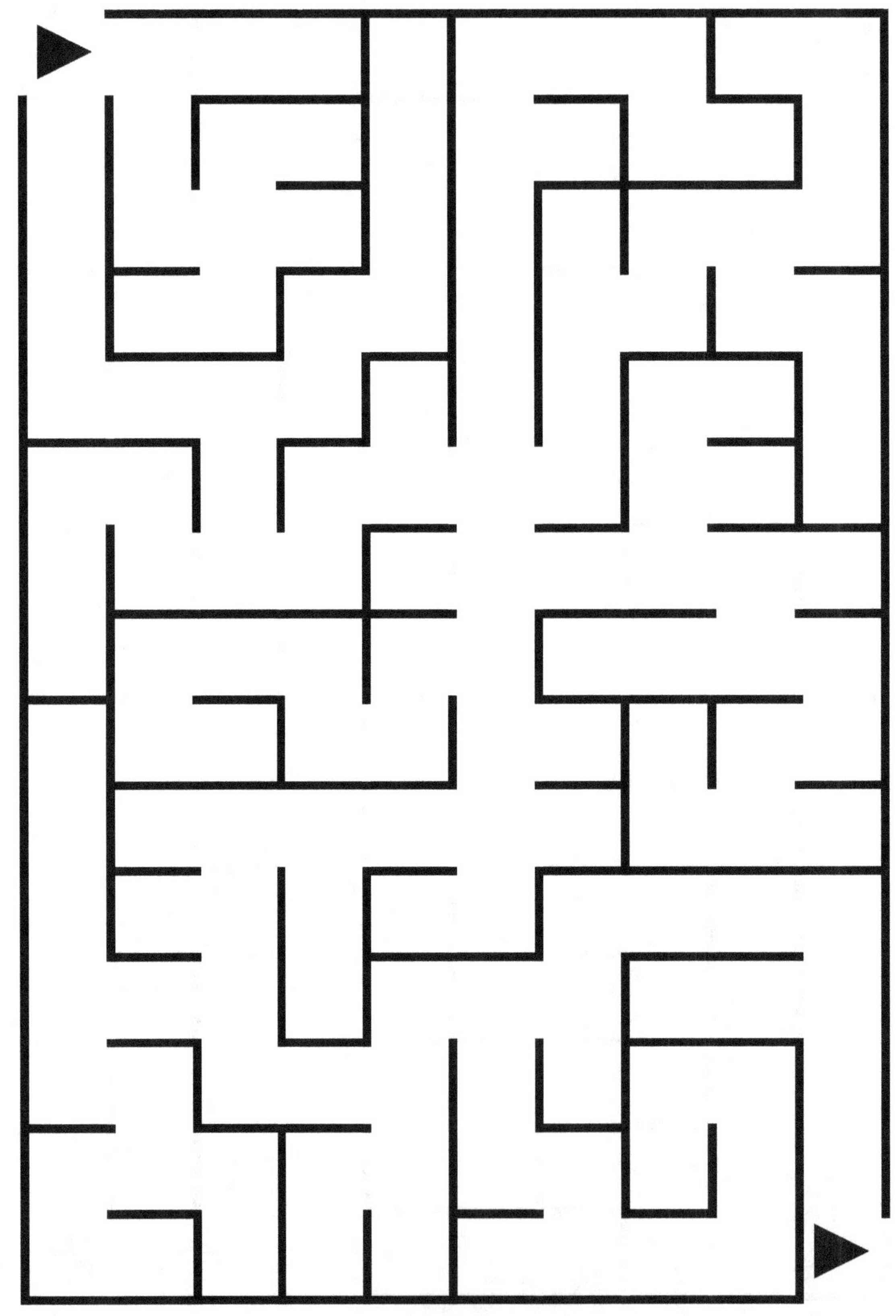

puzzle 78

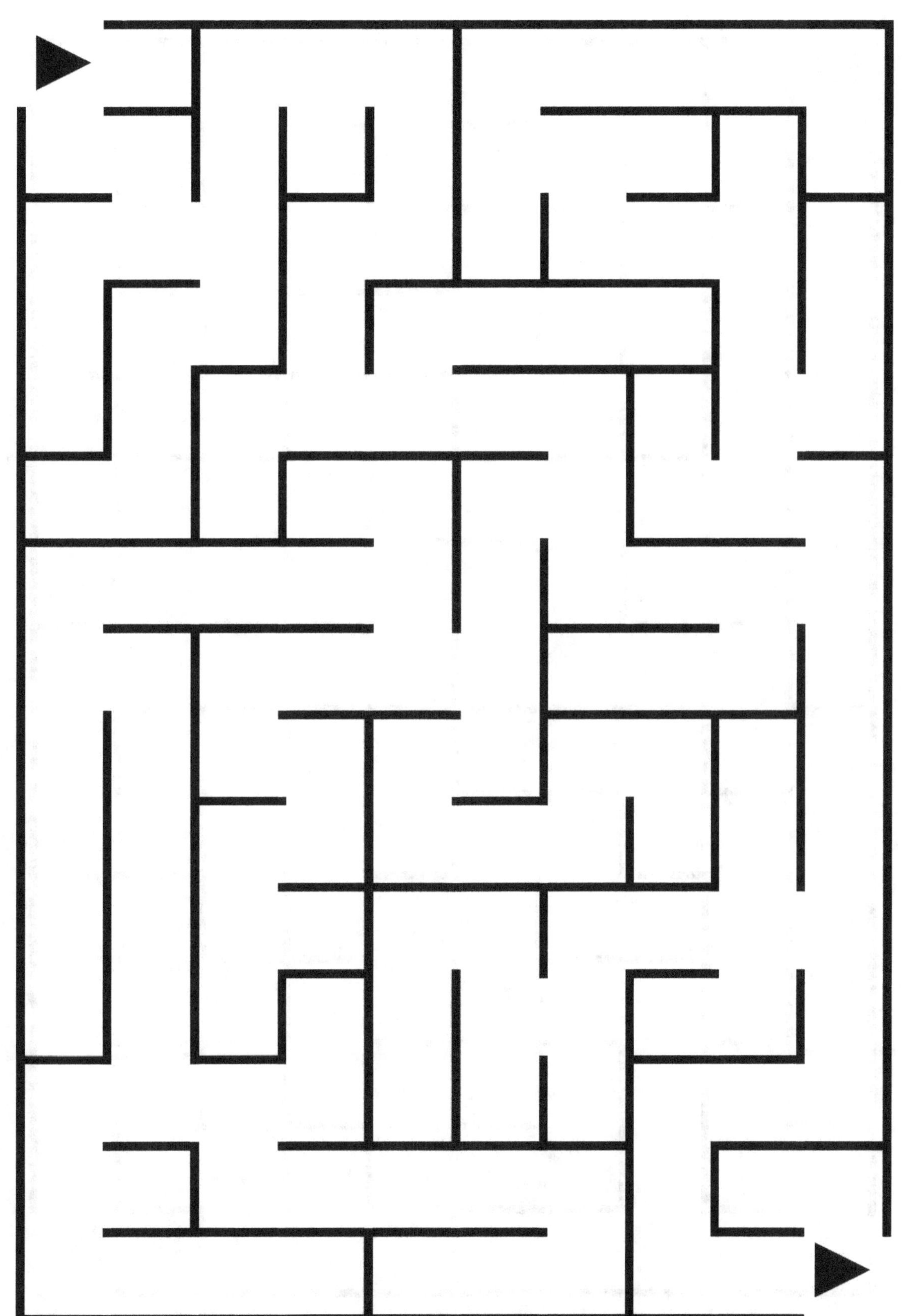

puzzle 79

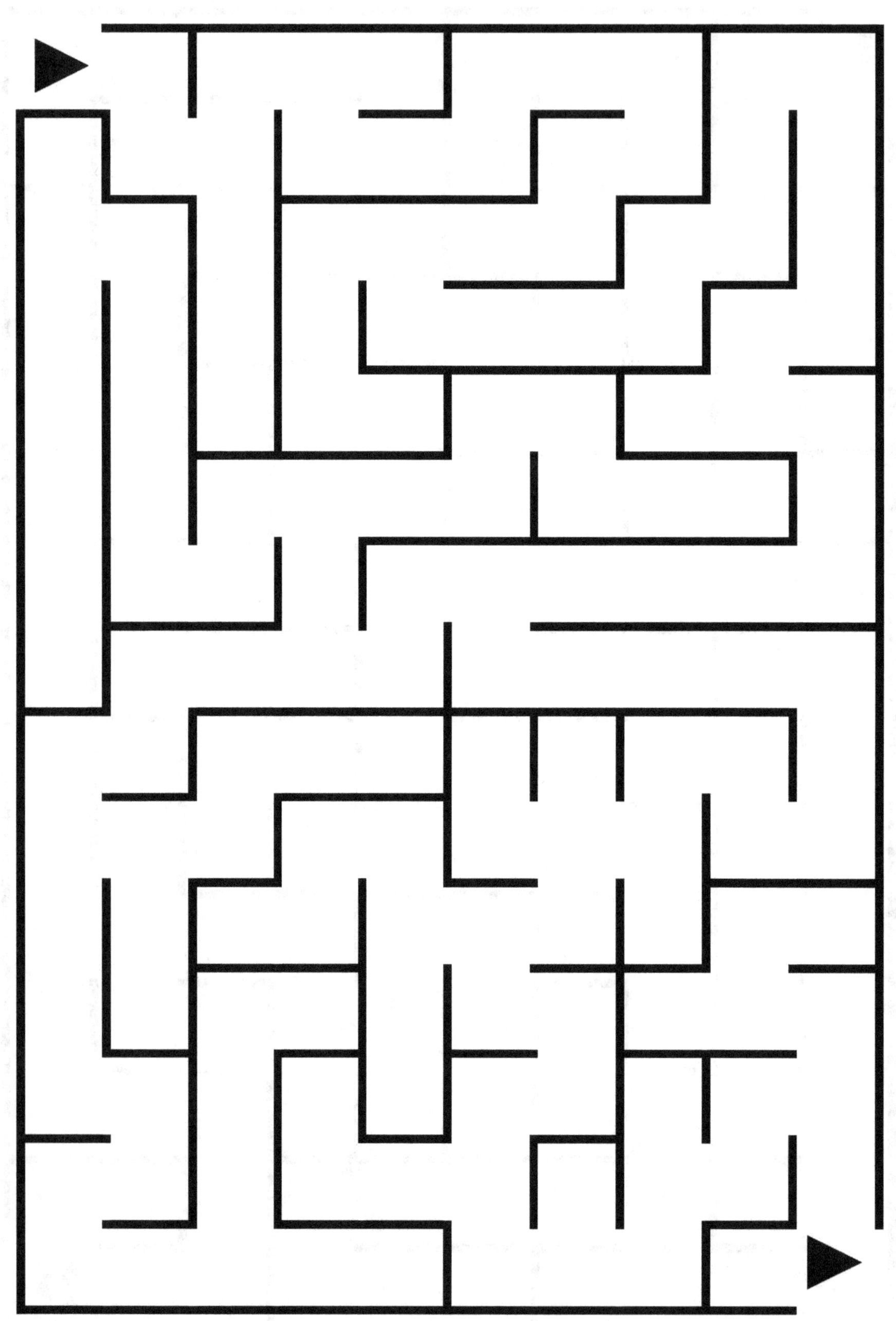

puzzle 80

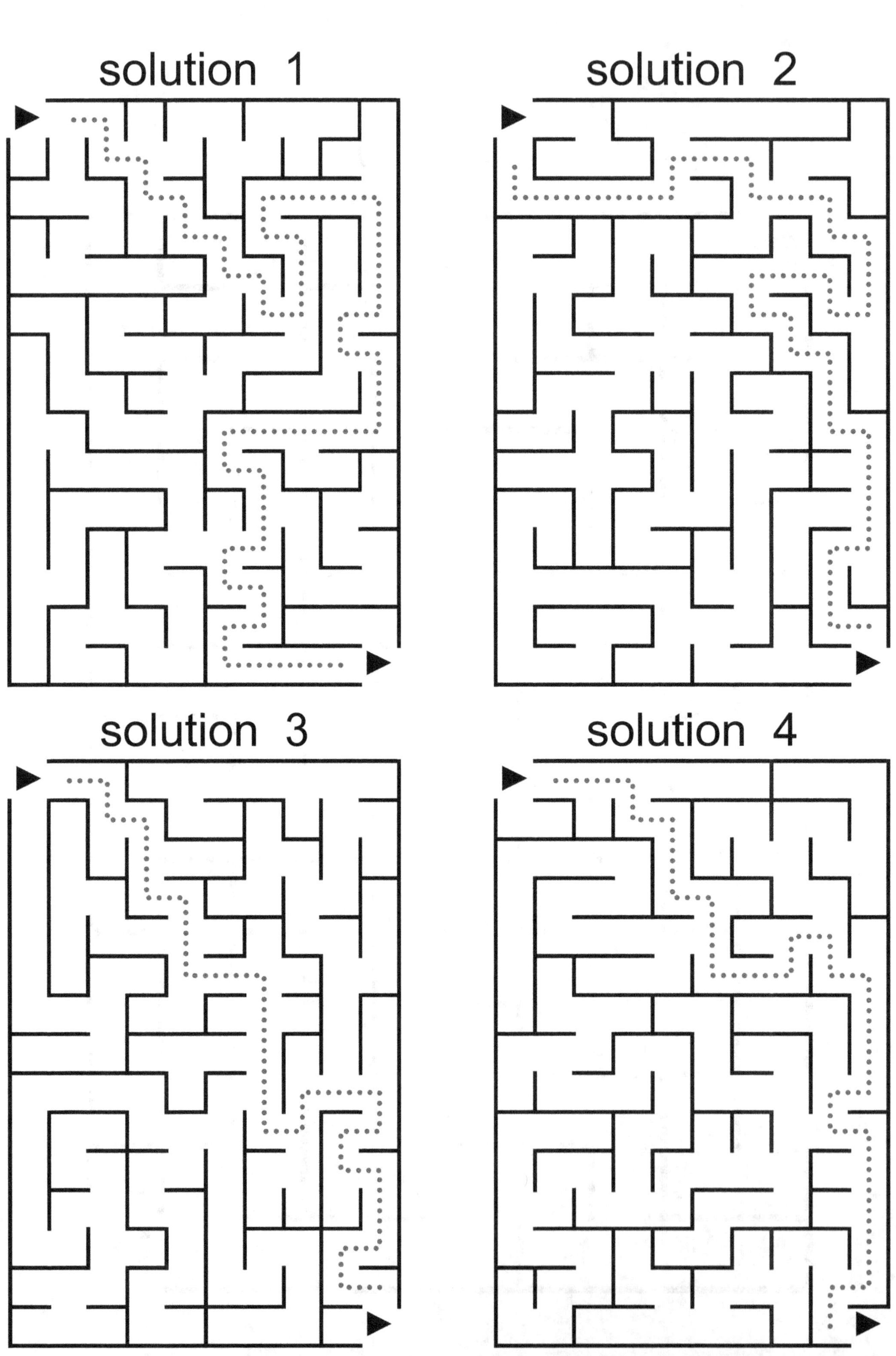

solution 1
solution 2
solution 3
solution 4

solution 5

solution 6

solution 7

solution 8

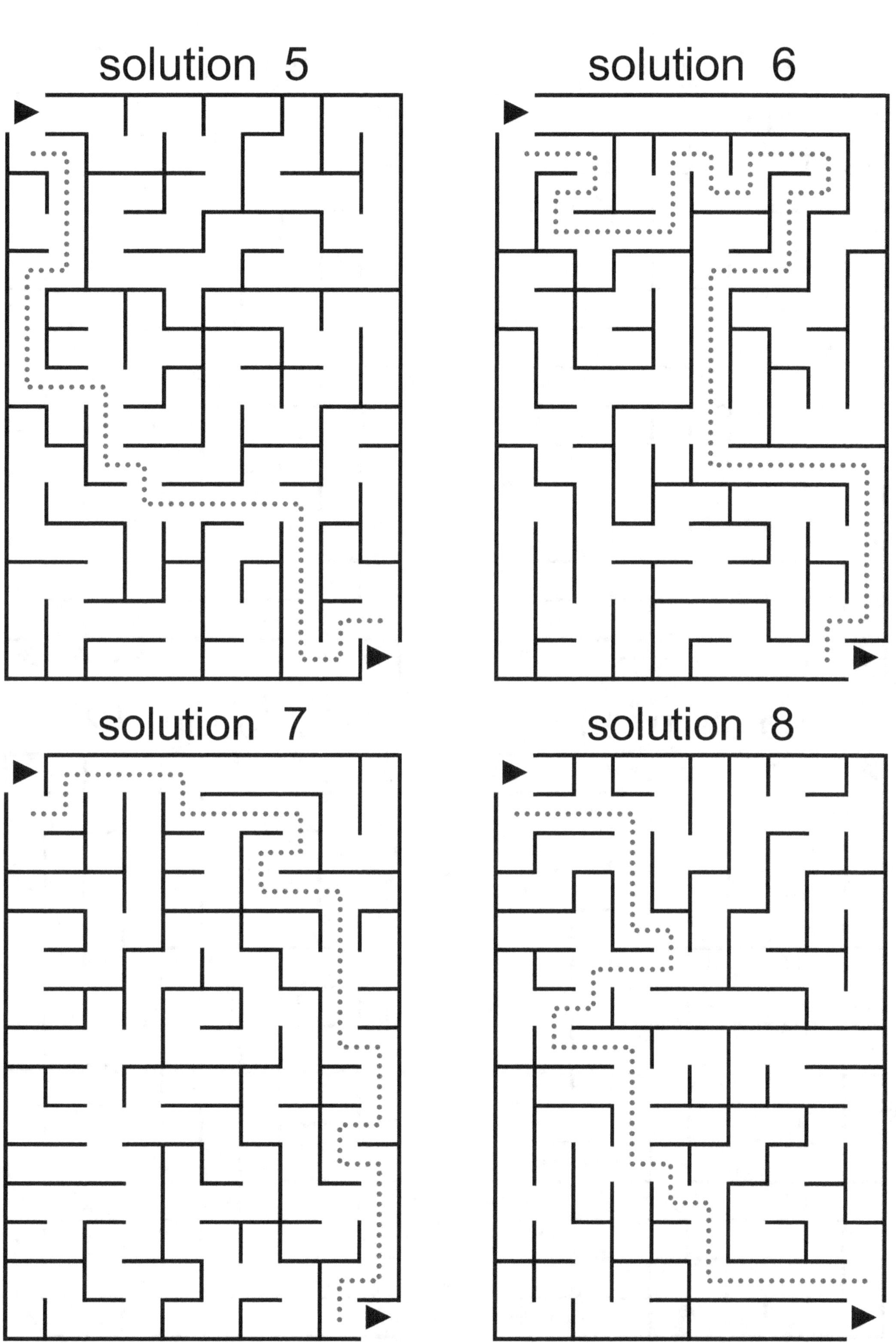

solution 9

solution 10

solution 11

solution 12

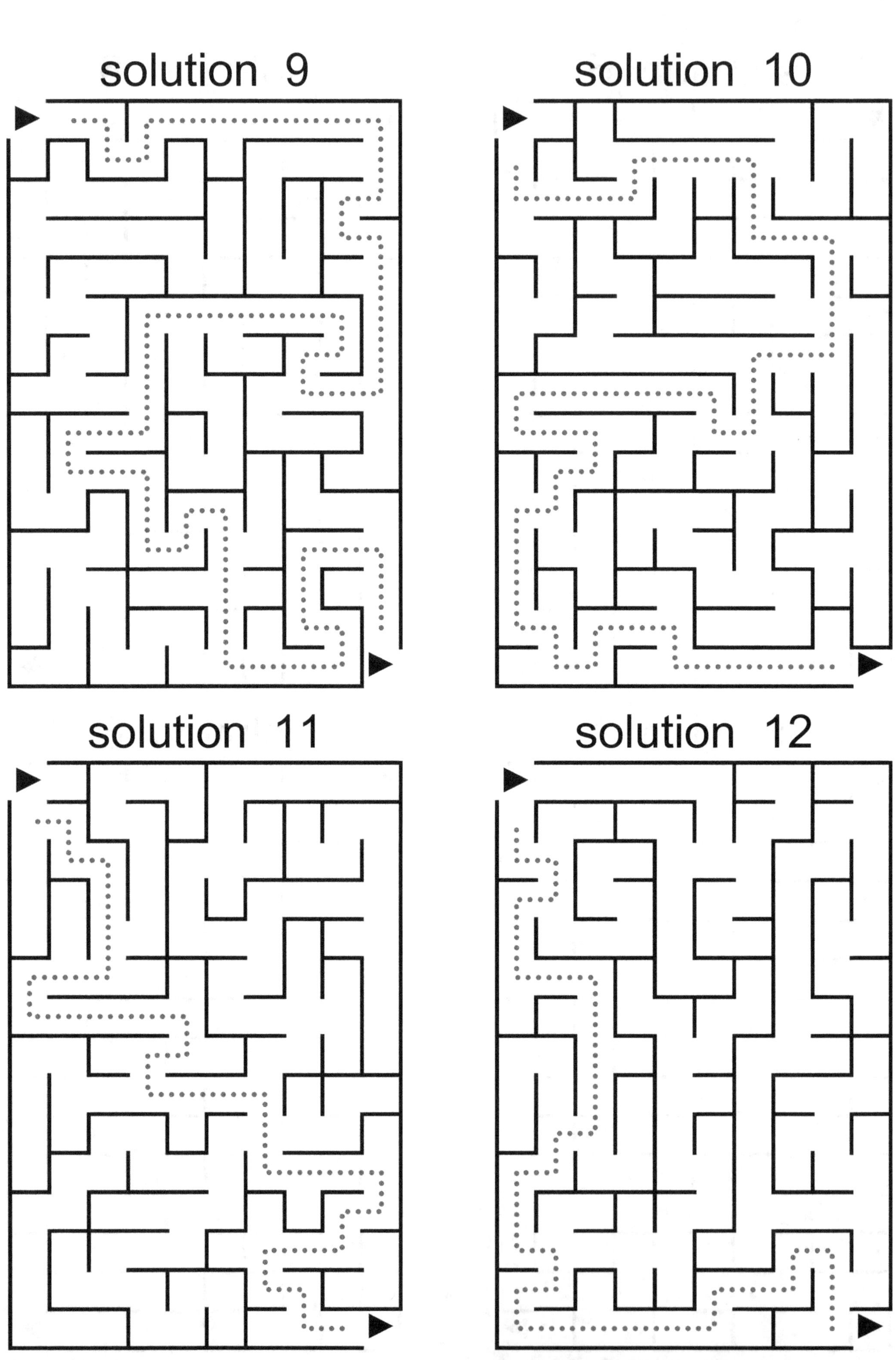

solution 13   solution 14

solution 15   solution 16

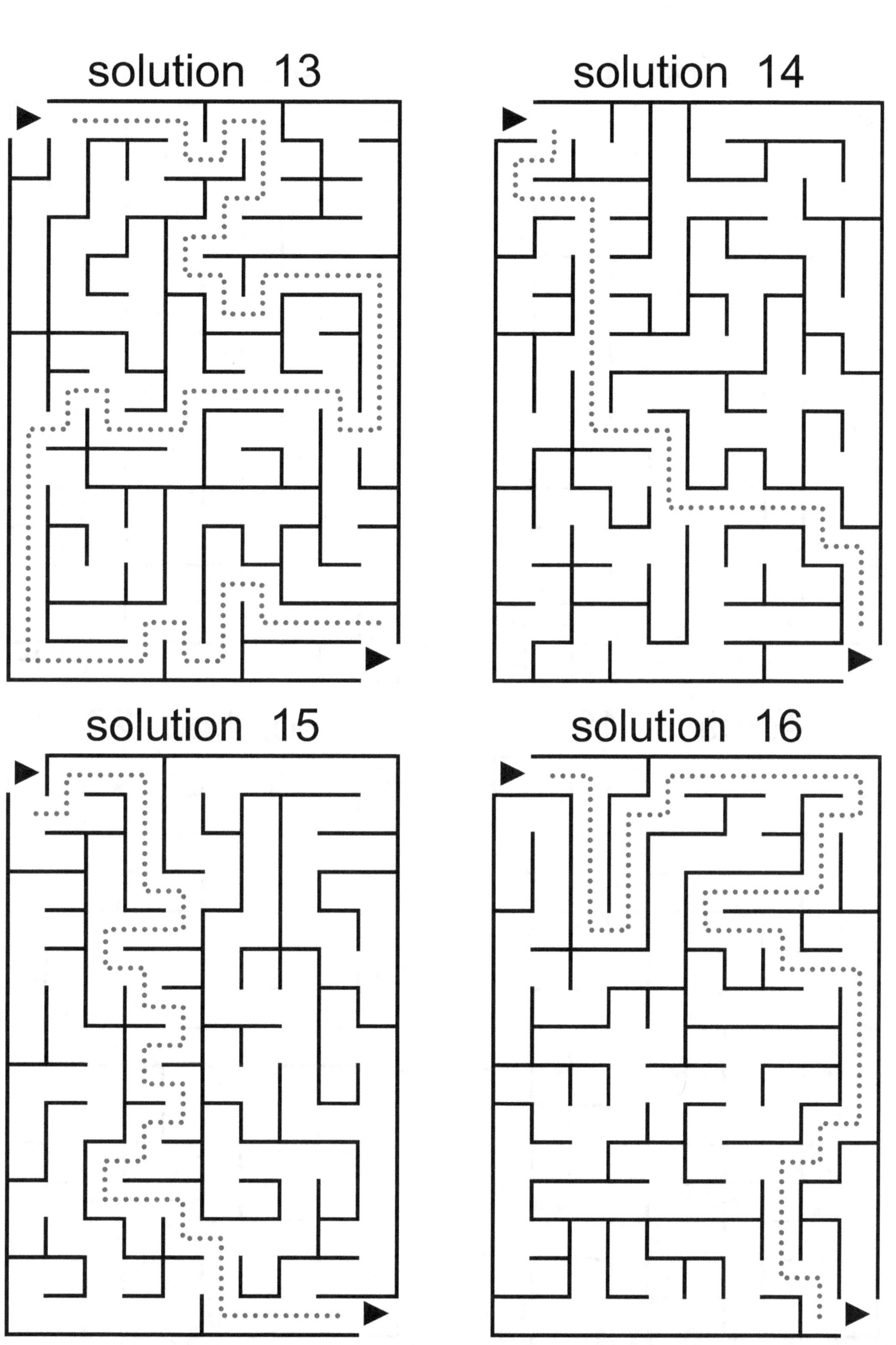

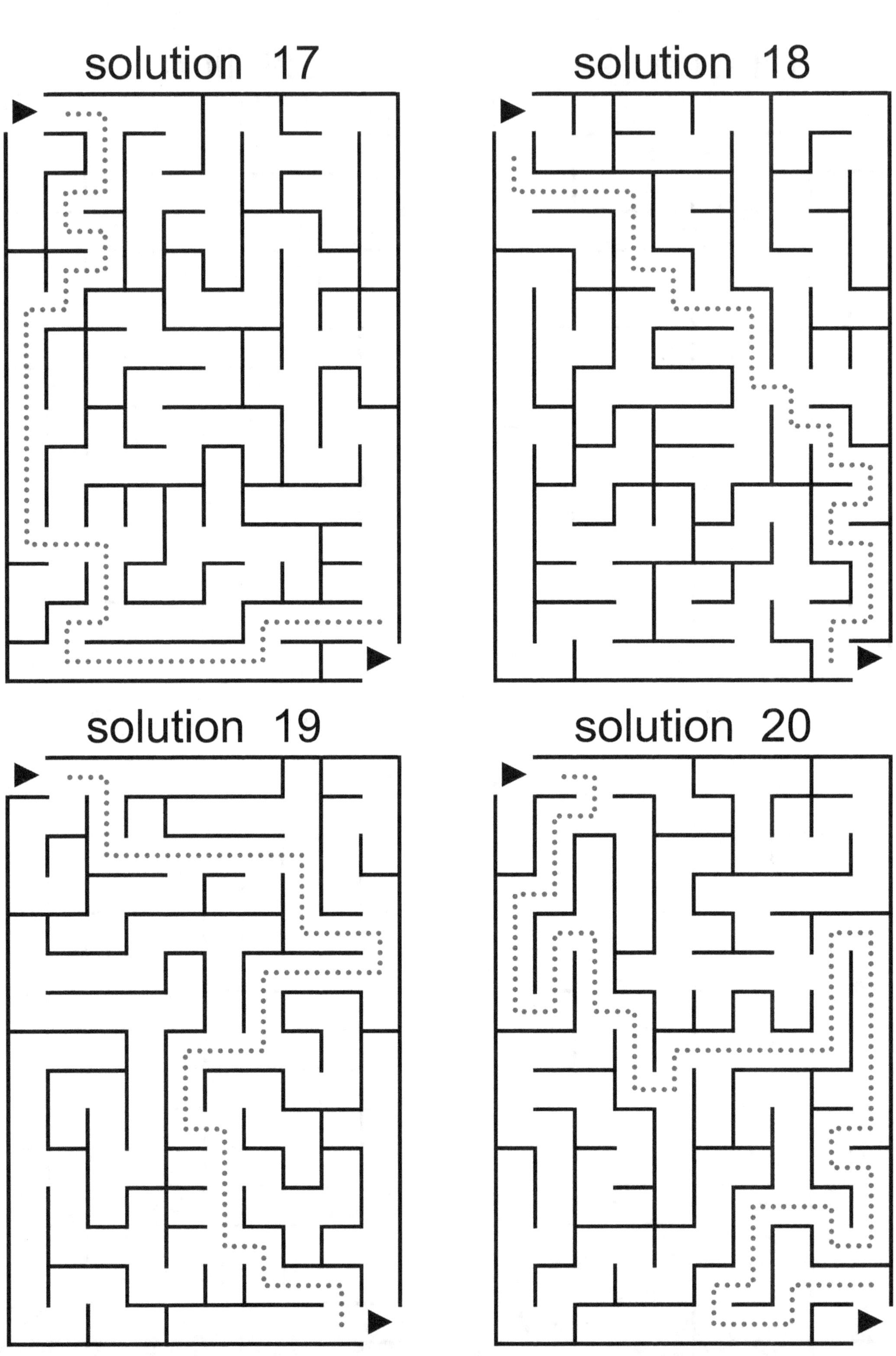

solution 17
solution 18
solution 19
solution 20

solution 21

solution 22

solution 23

solution 24

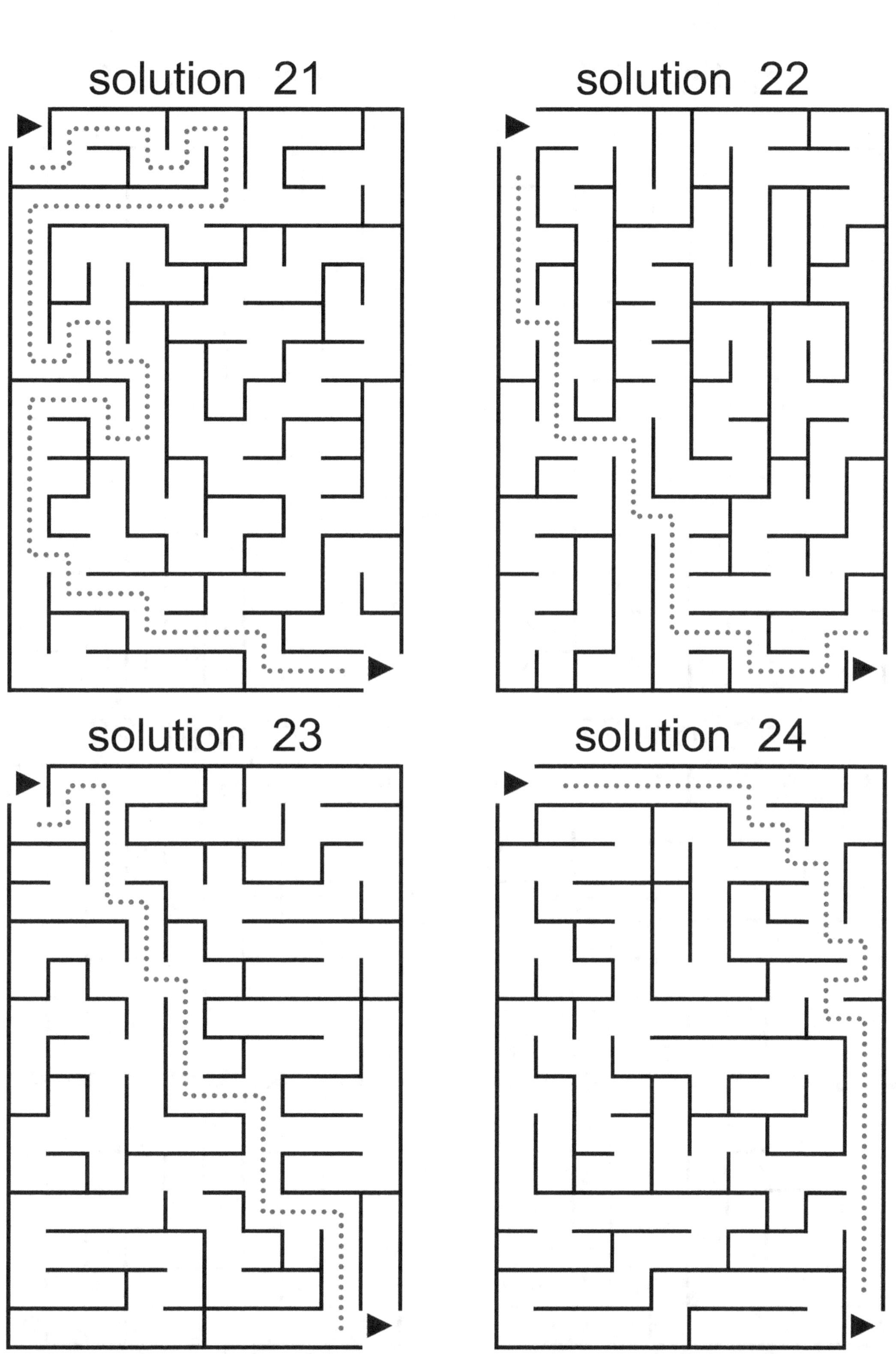

solution 25

solution 26

solution 27

solution 28

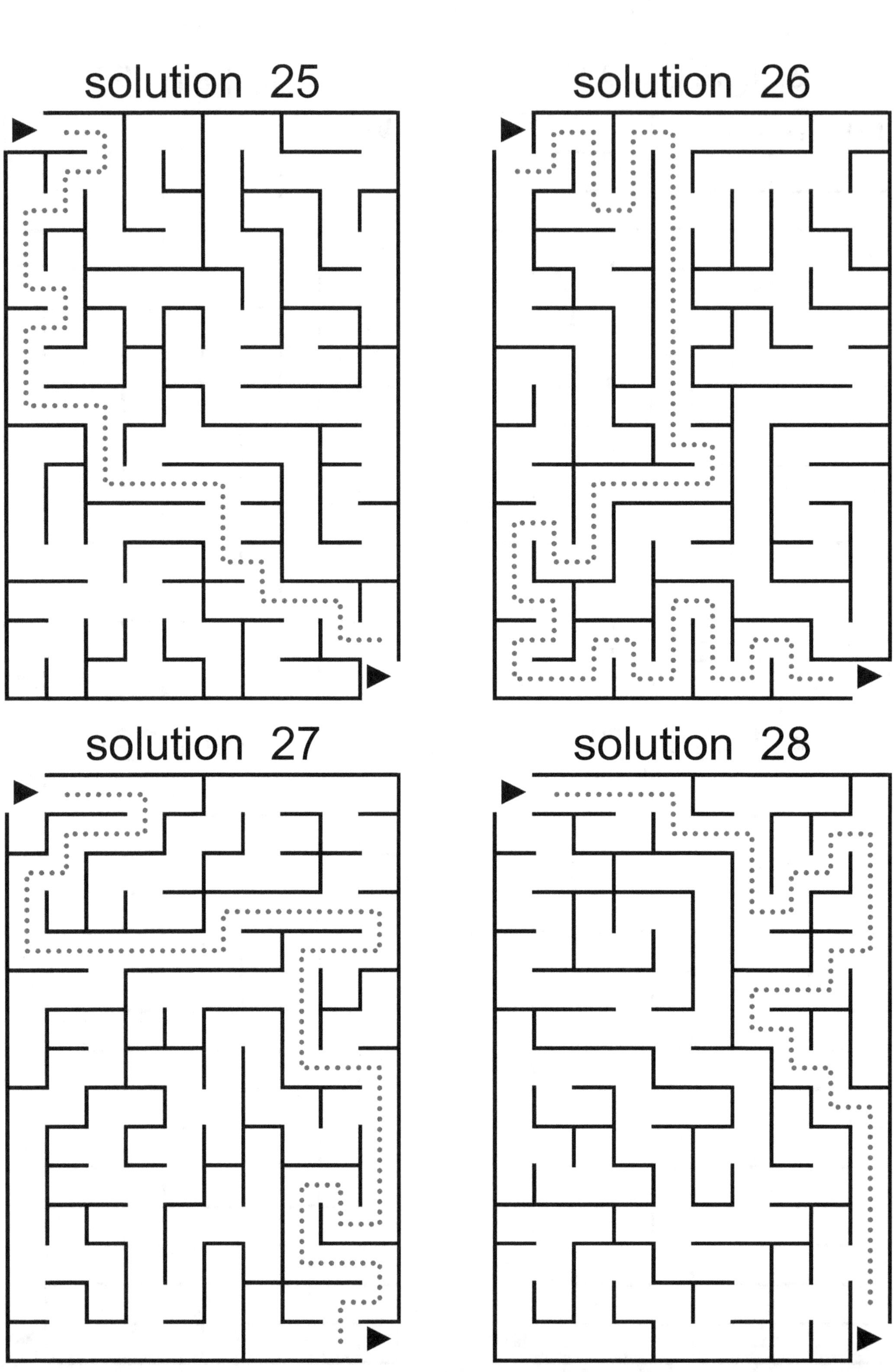

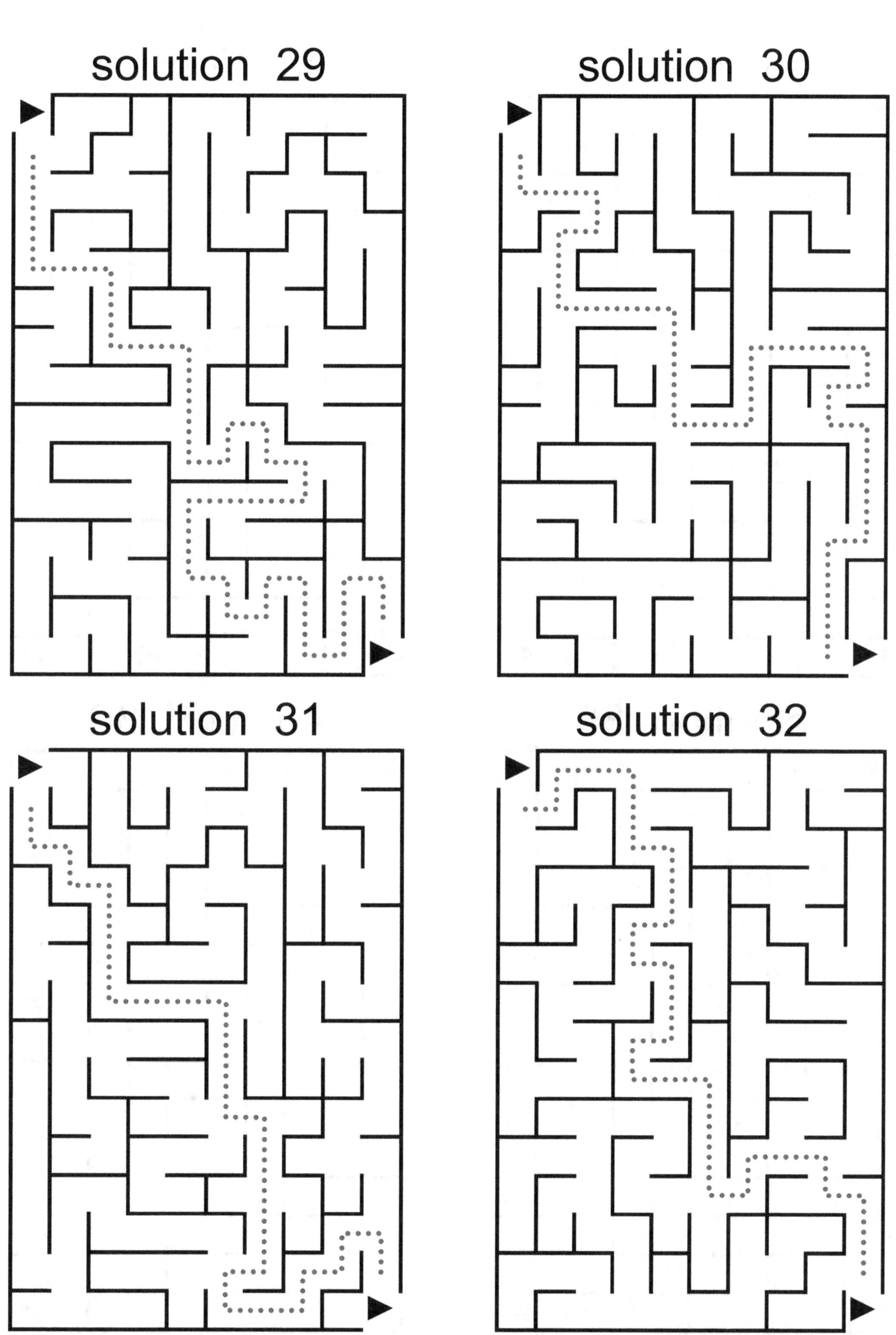

solution 29
solution 30
solution 31
solution 32

solution 33

solution 34

solution 35

solution 36

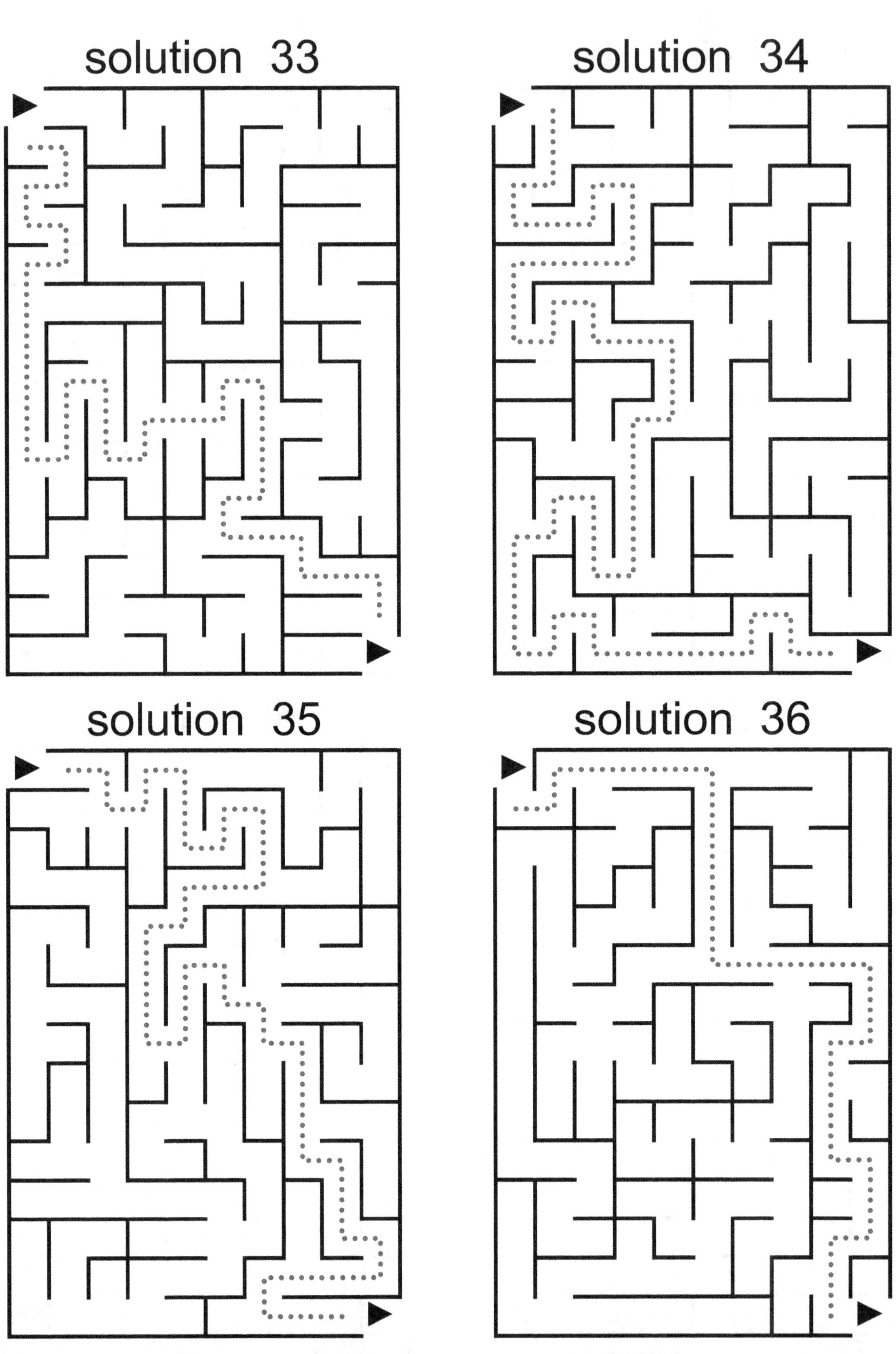

solution 37

solution 38

solution 39

solution 40

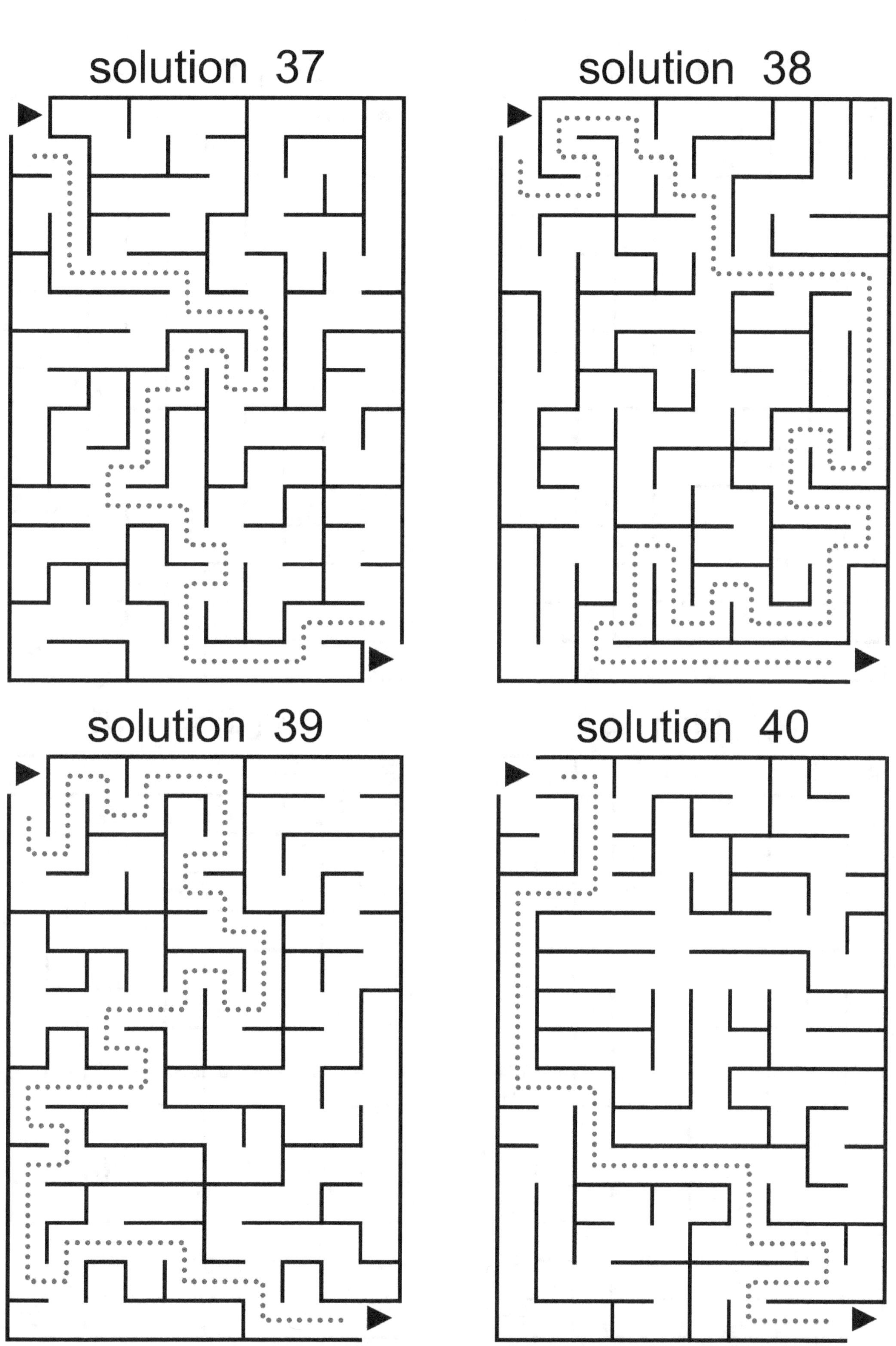

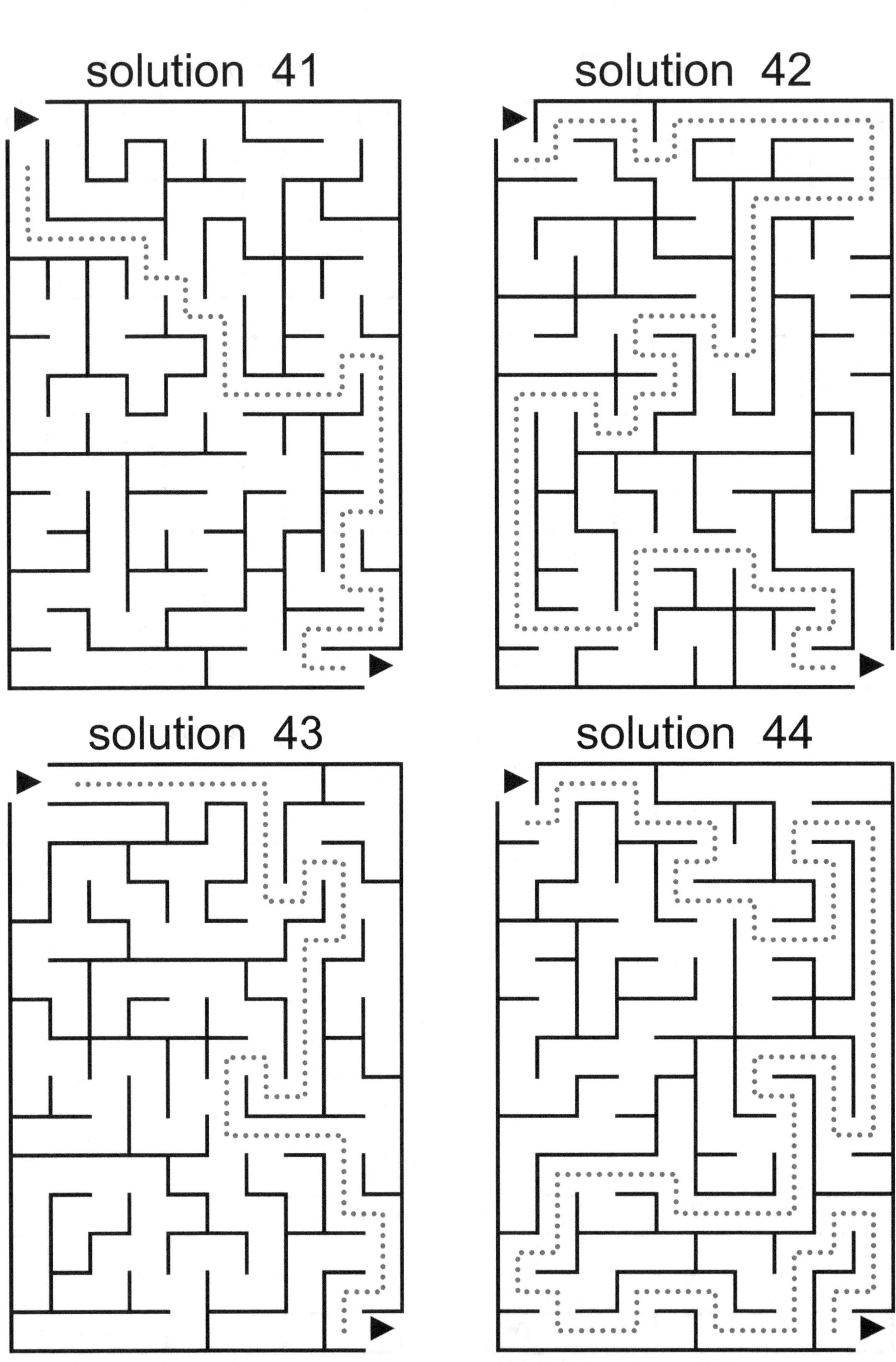

solution 41

solution 42

solution 43

solution 44

solution 45

solution 46

solution 47

solution 48

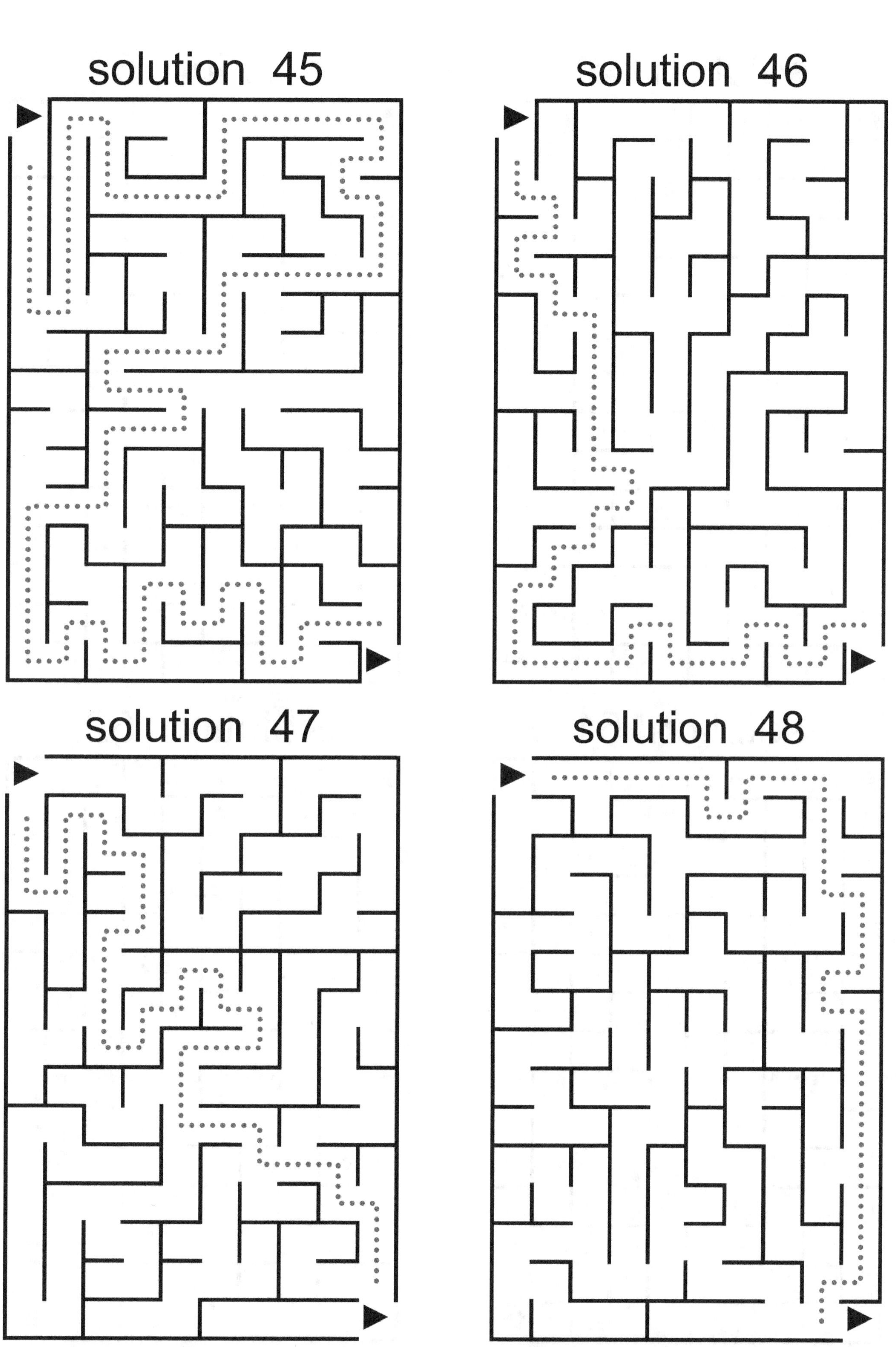

solution 49

solution 50

solution 51

solution 52

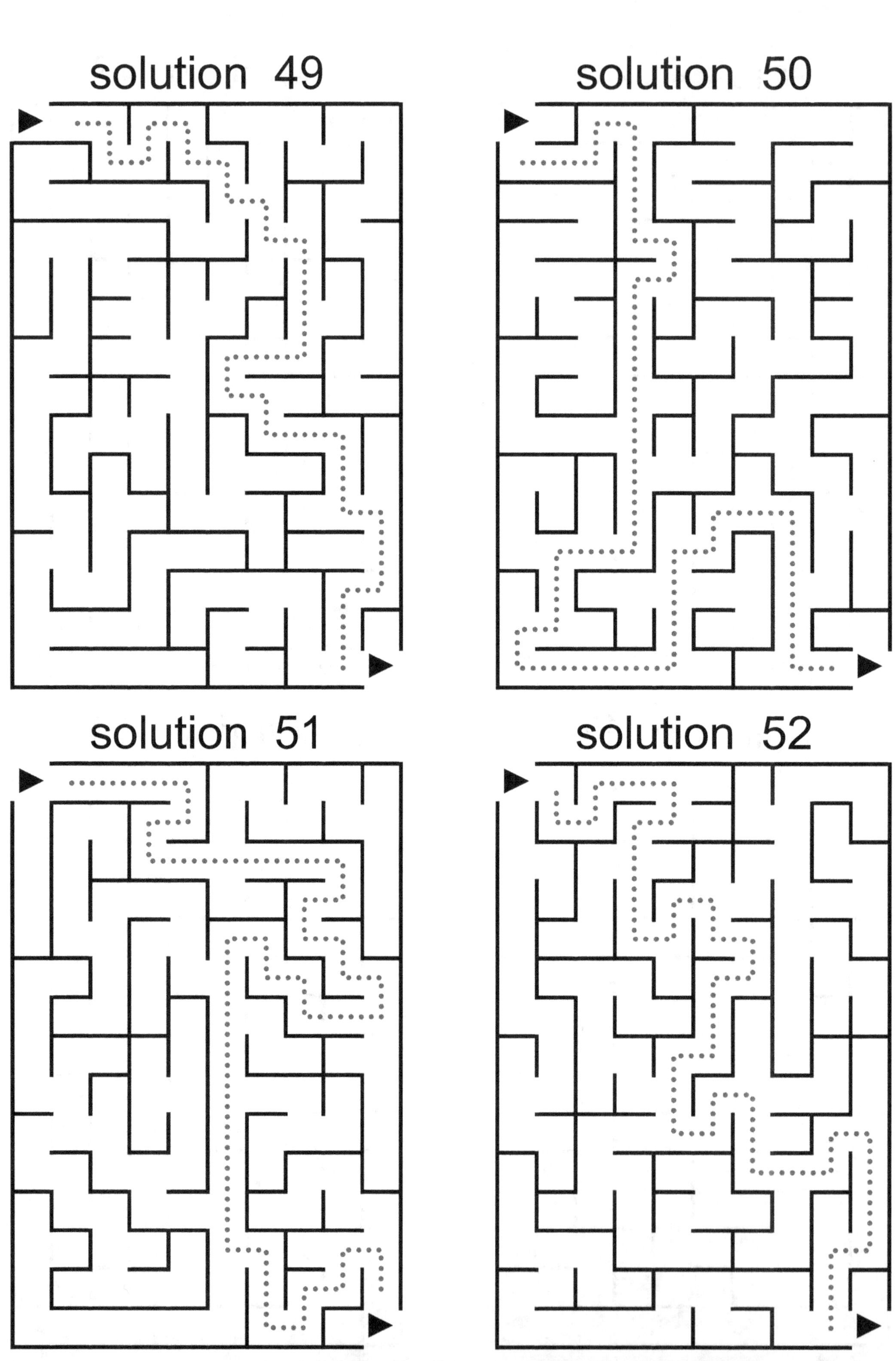

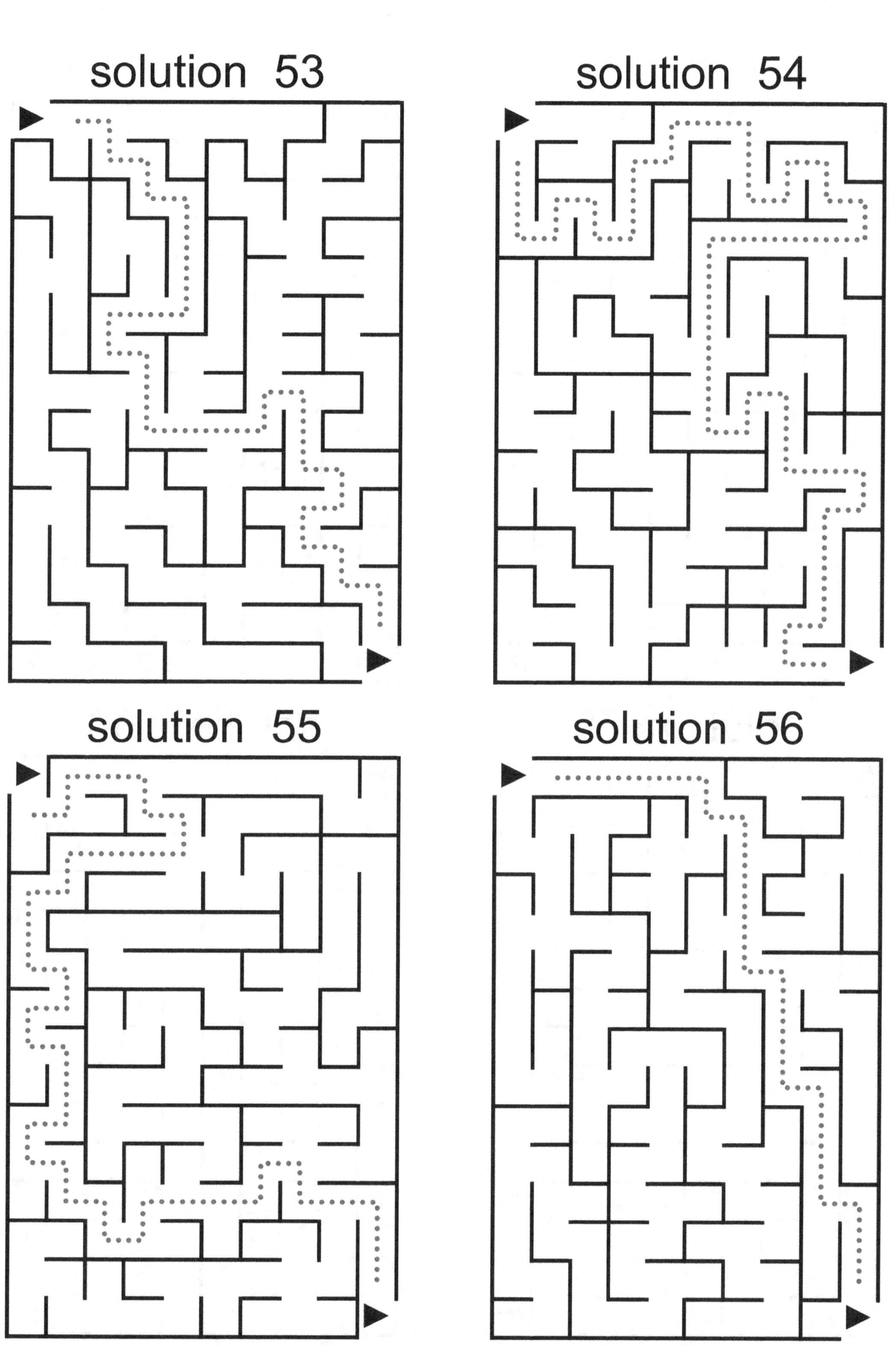

solution 53

solution 54

solution 55

solution 56

solution 57

solution 58

solution 59

solution 60

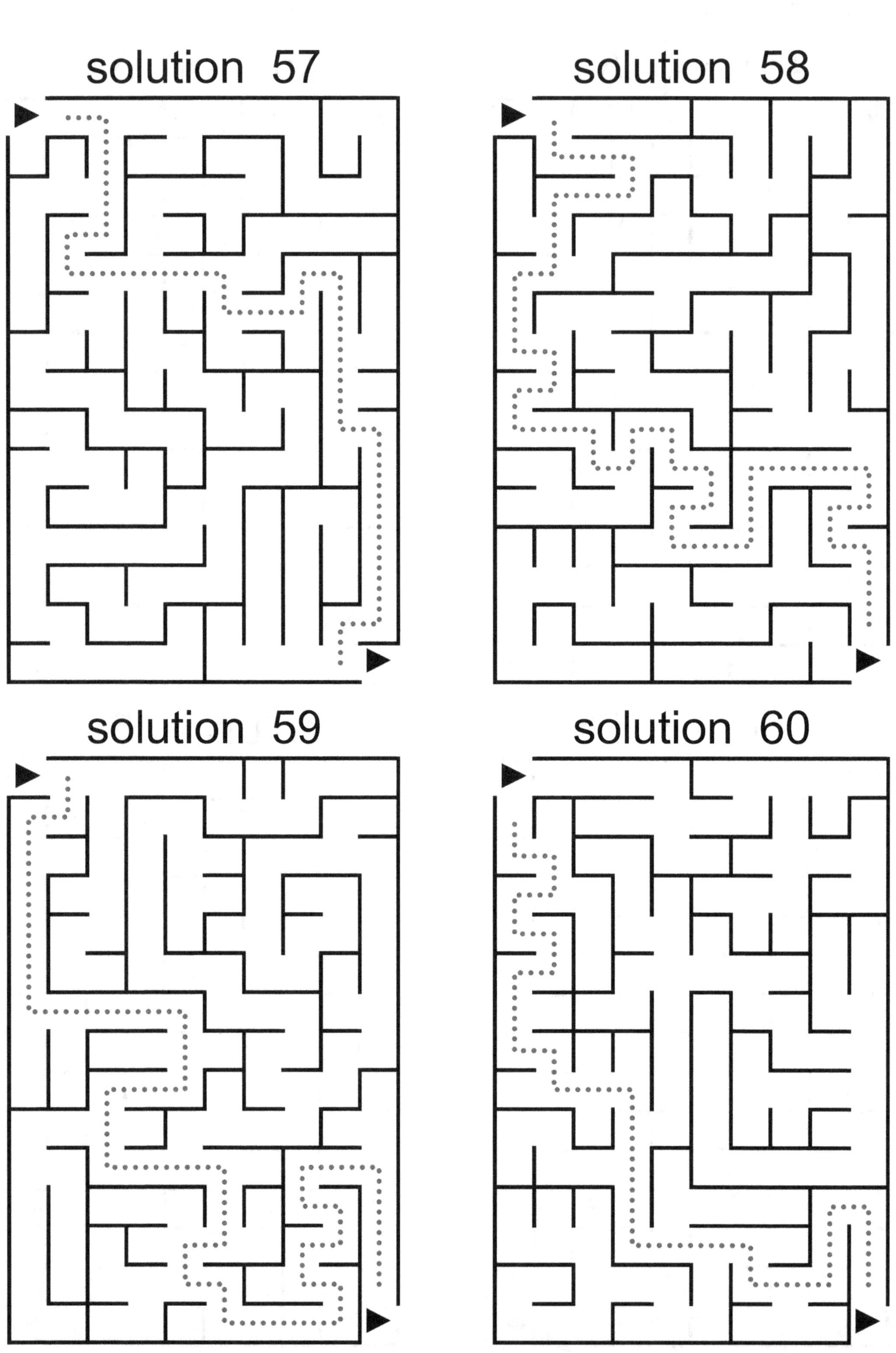

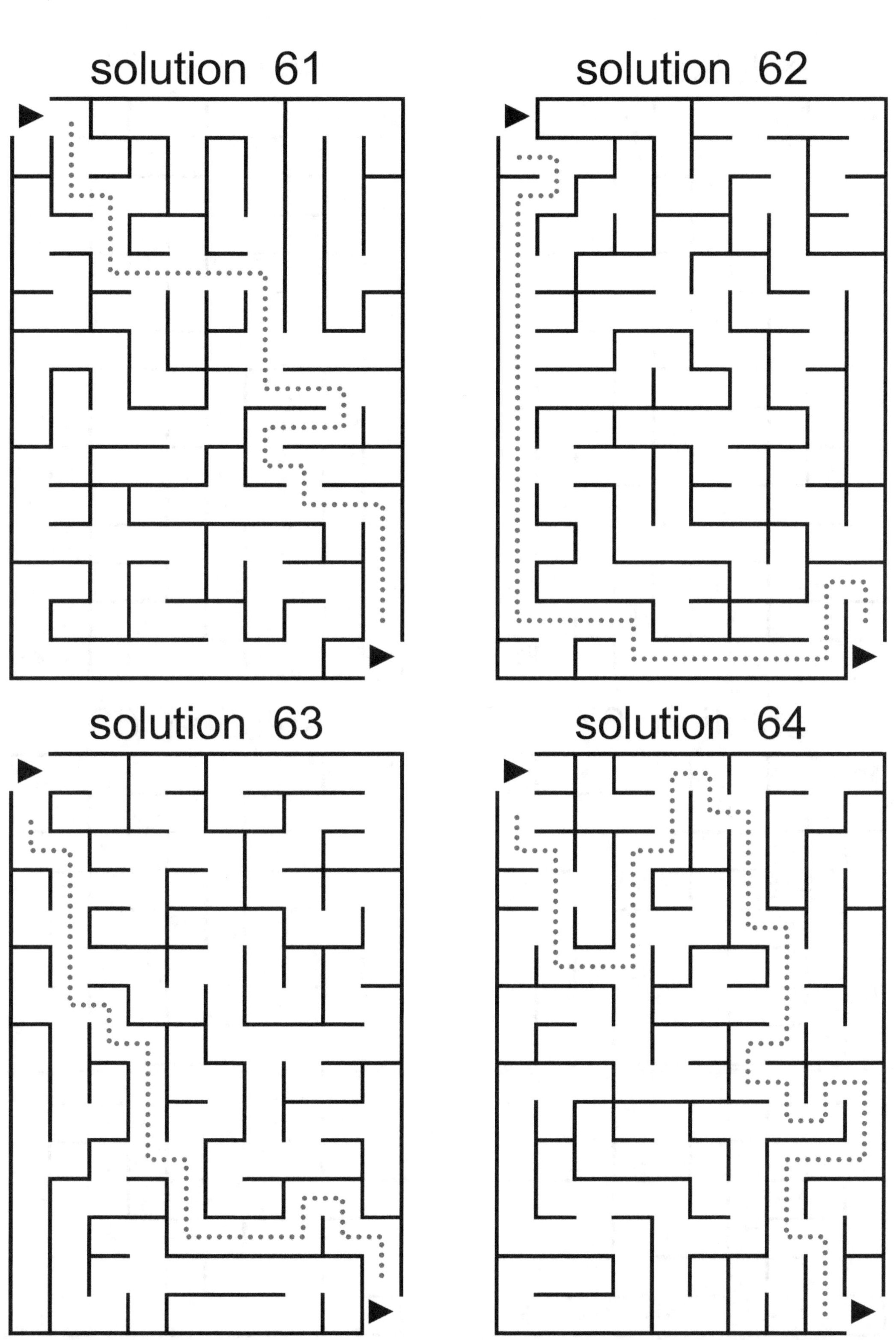

solution 61
solution 62
solution 63
solution 64

solution 65   solution 66

solution 67   solution 68

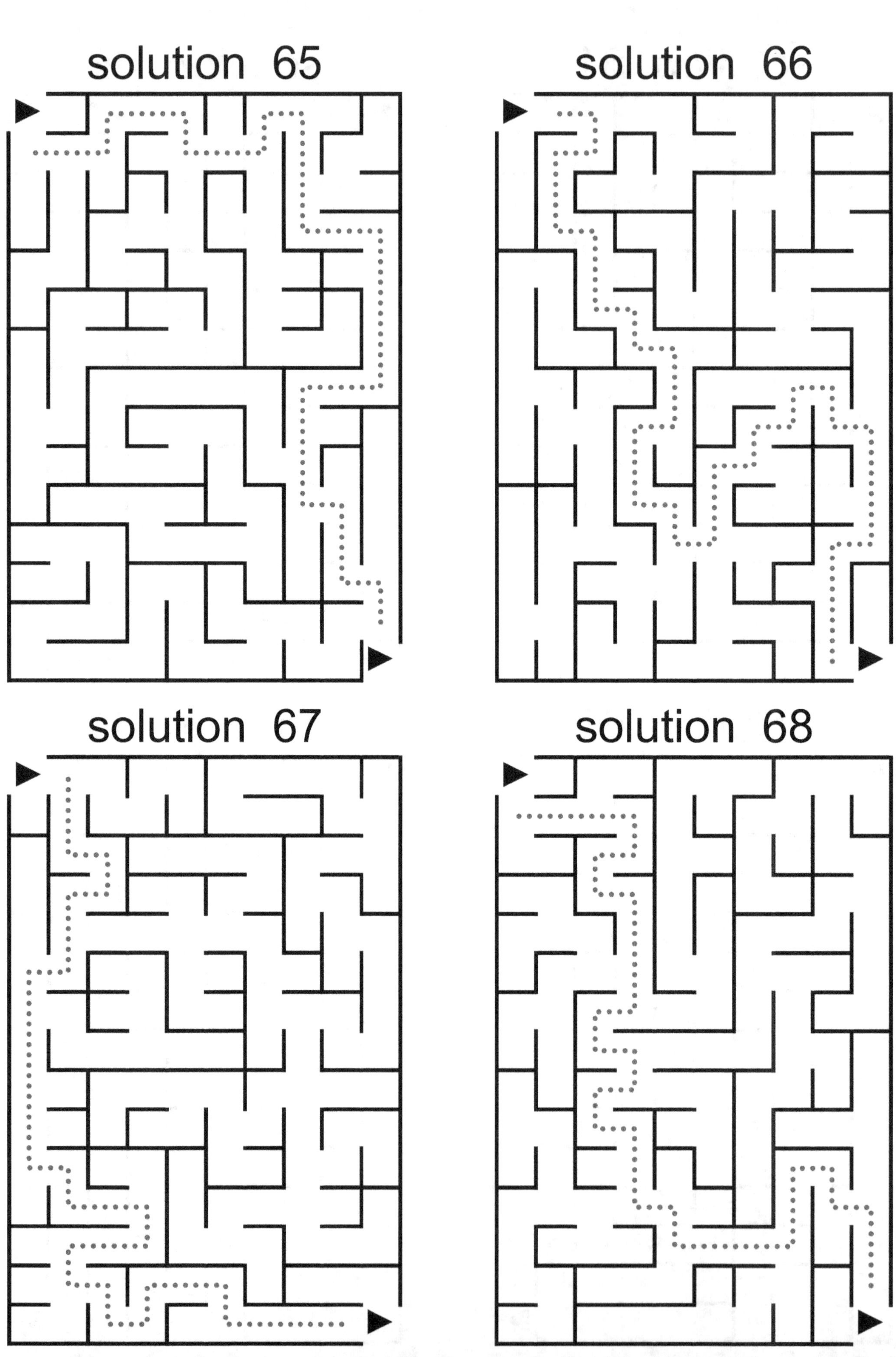

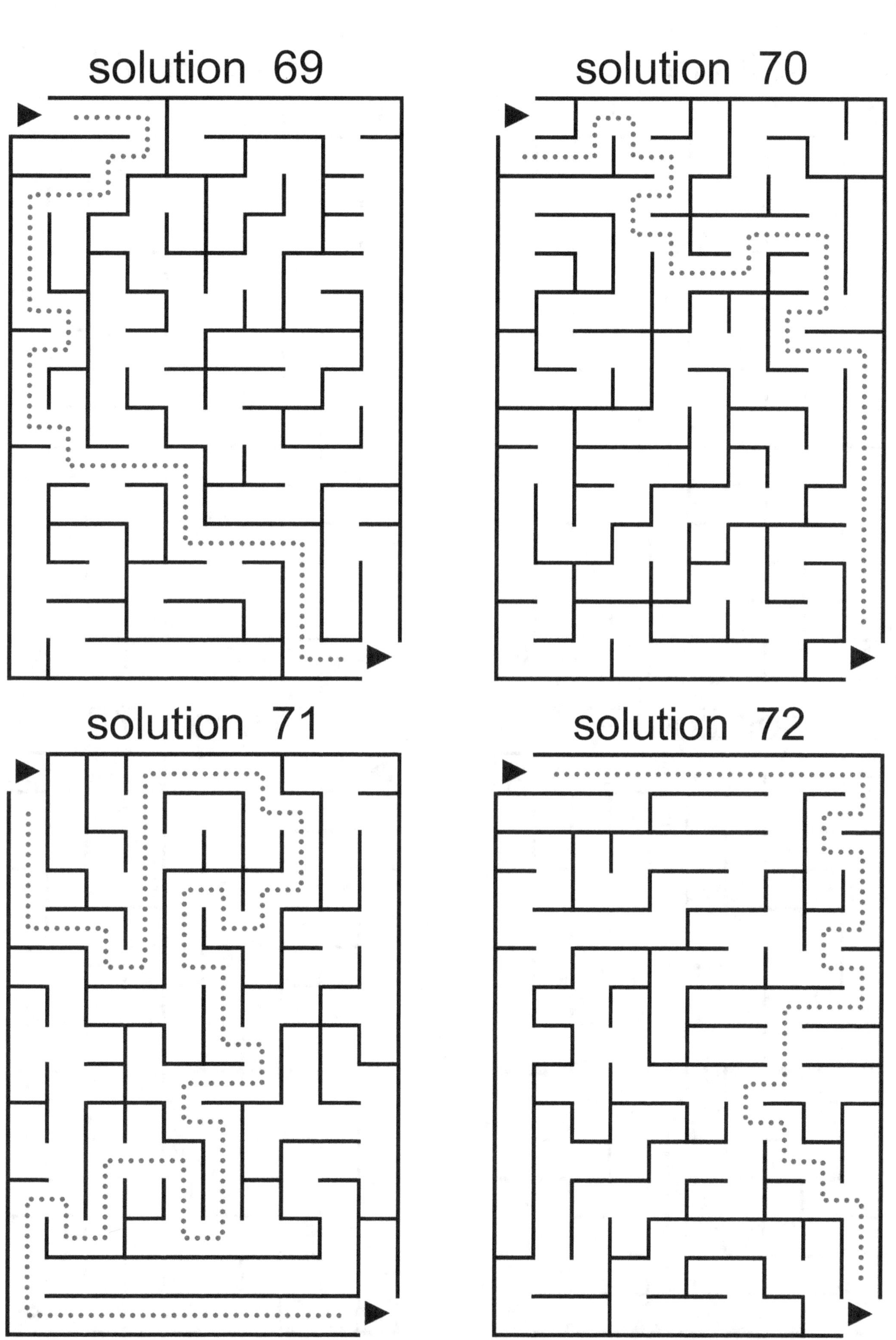

solution 69
solution 70
solution 71
solution 72

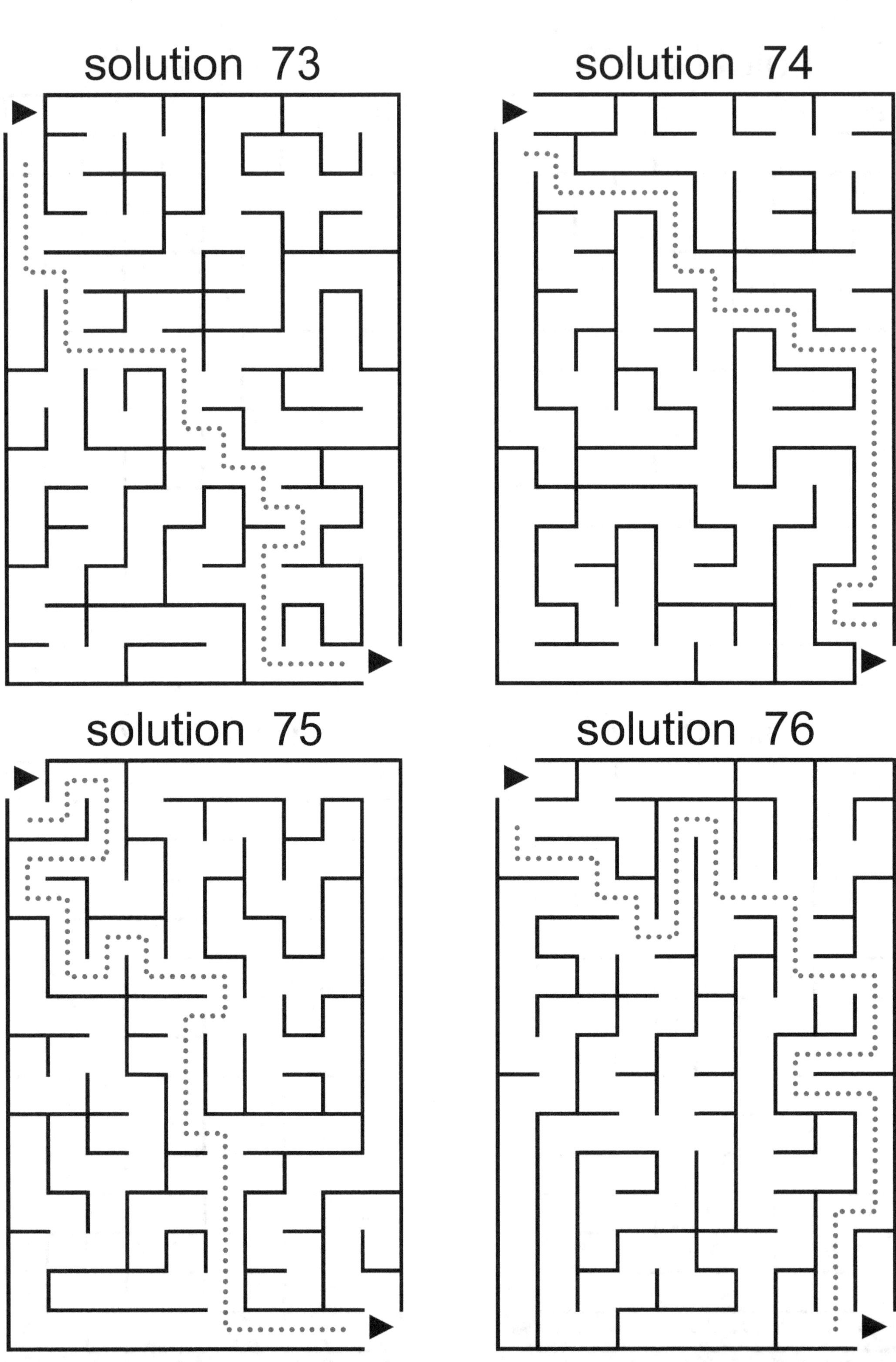

solution 73
solution 74
solution 75
solution 76

solution 77

solution 78

solution 79

solution 80

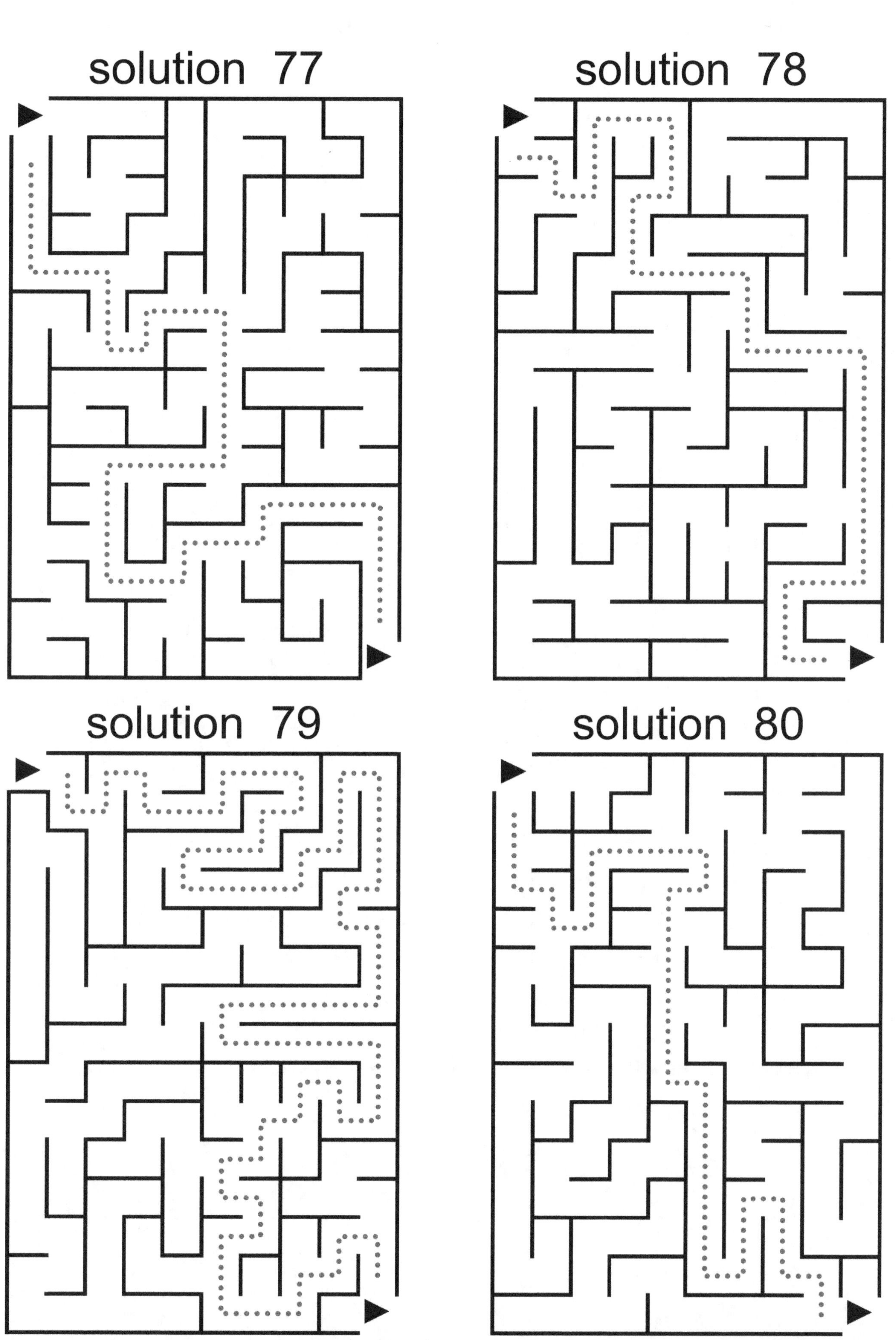